Short Stories of Kenji Miyazawa

Level 2
(1300-word)

Adapted by Nina Wegner

IBC パブリッシング

※本書の英文は IBC 対訳ライブラリー『英語で読む宮沢賢治短編集』と共通です。

はじめに

　ラダーシリーズは、「はしご（ladder）」を使って一歩一歩上を目指すように、学習者の実力に合わせ、無理なくステップアップできるよう開発された英文リーダーのシリーズです。

　リーディング力をつけるためには、繰り返したくさん読むこと、いわゆる「多読」がもっとも効果的な学習法であると言われています。多読では、「1. 速く 2. 訳さず英語のまま 3. なるべく辞書を使わず」に読むことが大切です。スピードを計るなど、速く読むよう心がけましょう（たとえば TOEIC® テストの音声スピードはおよそ 1 分間に 150 語です）。そして 1 語ずつ訳すのではなく、英語を英語のまま理解するくせをつけるようにします。こうして読み続けるうちに語感がついてきて、だんだんと英語が理解できるようになるのです。まずは、ラダーシリーズの中からあなたのレベルに合った本を選び、少しずつ英文に慣れ親しんでください。たくさんの本を手にとるうちに、英文書がすらすら読めるようになってくるはずです。

《本シリーズの特徴》
- 中学校レベルから中級者レベルまで5段階に分かれています。自分に合ったレベルからスタートしてください。
- クラシックから現代文学、ノンフィクション、ビジネスと幅広いジャンルを扱っています。あなたの興味に合わせてタイトルを選べます。
- 巻末のワードリストで、いつでもどこでも単語の意味を確認できます。レベル1、2では、文中の全ての単語が、レベル3以上は中学校レベル外の単語が掲載されています。
- カバーにヘッドホーンマークのついているタイトルは、オーディオ・サポートがあります。ウェブから購入／ダウンロードし、リスニング教材としても併用できます。

《使用語彙について》
レベル1：中学校で学習する単語約1000語
レベル2：レベル1の単語＋使用頻度の高い単語約300語
レベル3：レベル1の単語＋使用頻度の高い単語約600語
レベル4：レベル1の単語＋使用頻度の高い単語約1000語
レベル5：語彙制限なし

Contents

Gorsch the Cellist 1

The Police Chief 41

The Restaurant of Many Orders 57

The Wild Cat and the Acorns 81

Word List 106

Gorsch the Cellist

へたくそなセロ弾きの
ゴーシュは、いつも楽長に怒
られてばかり。もうすぐ町の公会
堂で行われる演奏会のため、ゴーシュ
は毎晩おそくまで練習をしている。あ
る晩、猫がやってきて、『トロイメライ』
を弾いてみろという。「いまいましい猫
め！」その晩から、さまざまな動物た
ちがゴーシュを訪ね、セロを弾くよ
うにと求めるようになる。しぶし
ぶ付き合っていたゴーシュ
であったが……。

読みはじめる前に

Gorsch the Cellist に出てくる語です。あらかじめ確認しておきましょう。

- ☐ cellist　　　　チェロ奏者
- ☐ cello　　　　チェロ
- ☐ conductor　　指揮者
- ☐ symphony　　交響曲
- ☐ clap　　　　（手を）たたく
- ☐ flat　　　　単調な
- ☐ scale　　　　音階
- ☐ line　　　　小節
- ☐ music　　　　楽譜
- ☐ Schumann　　ロベルト・シューマン《ドイツの作曲家。1810–1856》
- ☐ Träumerei　　トロイメライ（夢）《シューマンのピアノ曲集「子供の情景」の第7曲》
- ☐ note　　　　音色、音符
- ☐ off　　　　調子が悪い
- ☐ cuckoo　　　カッコウ
- ☐ badger　　　アナグマ
- ☐ in time　　　正しいテンポで
- ☐ string　　　弦
- ☐ bow　　　　お辞儀をする、弓
- ☐ circulation　血行
- ☐ instrument　楽器
- ☐ encore　　　アンコール

Gorsch was known as the man who played the cello at the theater in town. Sadly, everybody knew he was not a very good musician. But maybe the words "not very good" were too kind. The truth was that Gorsch was a bad cello player. In fact, he was probably the worst musician in the orchestra. The conductor was always getting mad at him for it.

One day, Gorsch and the other musicians were practicing the Sixth Symphony at the theater. They were going to play the Sixth Symphony at the town hall soon.

The trumpets sounded heroic. The

clarinets sounded lovely. The violins sounded fine, playing hard and fast.

Gorsch played his cello just as hard as all the others. He saw and heard nothing else but the music written on the paper in front of him. His mouth was shut tight. His eyes were wide open as he read the music.

Suddenly, the conductor clapped his hands.

The musicians stopped playing.

"Gorsch! You're late!" the conductor shouted. "The cello must come in at *tah-tah-tee-dum*! Understand? Everyone, start again at *tah-tah-tee-dum*!"

Gorsch's face turned red. But they all started again. By trying very, very hard, Gorsch got safely through the difficult part. He started playing the next part feeling more sure of himself. But just then the conductor clapped his hands again.

"Gorsch! You're too flat! You must get it right! I don't have time to teach you the simple scale, you know!"

Most of the other musicians looked away. Some busily read the music in front of them. They all felt sorry for Gorsch.

"All right, let's take it from the line before."

They all began to play again. This time, they got quite far without having to stop. Gorsch played with all his might. But right when he was feeling rather pleased, the conductor clapped his hands again.

"Oh, no! Not again," Gorsch thought.

But this time the conductor yelled at somebody else. Gorsch was glad that it wasn't him this time. As the conductor yelled, Gorsch read his music and tried to look busy, just as the others had done for him.

"All right, let's just get through the next bit," the conductor said.

Again, they started playing. But as soon as they started, the conductor gave a great, angry clap and started yelling.

"Oh, this is terrible! This is the most important part of the piece and you're doing it all wrong! We only have ten days until we play the Sixth Symphony. We're supposed to be great musicians! But here we are sounding like a group of children! Gorsch, you're the main problem. You don't play with any *feeling*, and you're always too slow. We can't keep going like this. It's not right for everyone in the

Venus Orchestra to be held back by one man. You must do better."

The conductor looked down and shook his head.

"That's enough for now," he said. "Get some rest and be back here at six o'clock."

The musicians all packed up their things and left.

Holding onto his cheap cello, Gorsch turned to the wall and cried. Big tears rolled down his face. But soon, he sat up straight. He pulled himself together. Sitting there all alone, he began to play the part they had just finished.

Gorsch went home later that night carrying his big, black box on his back. He lived in a small, poor house by the river. It was just outside of town. Gorsch lived alone. He spent most of his mornings taking care of the vegetables in his small field. But every afternoon, Gorsch went out.

Inside the house, he opened the black box. Inside, of course, was the cello. Gorsch drank a glass of water. Then he sat down to play.

Gorsch played the piece of music he had practiced with the orchestra that day. He played the music with great energy, like a hungry lion.

As he turned the pages of his music, he played and he thought. Then he thought and he played. Over and over again, he played the music from the beginning to the end. He didn't notice the time, and he played until long past midnight. In the end, he was so tired that his face was red and his eyes were heavy with sleep.

Just then, somebody knocked three times at the door.

"Who is it?" he called out.

The door opened. In walked a large cat carrying a heavy tomato in its mouth. He set the tomato down in front of Gorsch.

"Phew!" said the cat. "Carrying heavy things is difficult."

"What on earth...!" said Gorsch in surprise.

"This is a present for you," said the cat.

This was all too much for Gorsch, who was already very tired. Suddenly, the anger and sadness that had been building up inside him all day came out all at once.

"Why would I want a tomato from

someone like you? And that tomato is from *my* field! Who do you think you are? You can't just take things from my field! Get out of here, you bad cat!"

At these words, the cat hung his head and looked sad. But, he tried to smile and said, "You shouldn't get so angry, Mr. Gorsch. It's not good for you. Maybe you should just play something instead of yelling. How about Schumann's 'Träumerei'? I'd love to hear that."

"I've never seen such a bad cat!" said Gorsch. He sat there angrily.

"Please play," said the cat. "I can't sleep unless I hear you play."

"That's enough out of you! Enough!" yelled Gorsch. His face was red. He clapped his hands angrily, just as the conductor had done earlier that day. But suddenly, he changed his mind.

"All right," he said darkly. "I'll play for you."

Gorsch went around the small house. He closed all the windows and locked the door. He turned off the lights. Then he sat down with his cello. He could now only see by the light of the moon that came in through the window.

"You want to hear 'Träumerei' by Schumann, right?" he said.

"Yes," said the cat, wiping his face.

"Is this how the song goes?" Gorsch asked. But he began to play a piece called "Tiger Hunt in India."

At first, the cat listened quietly with closed eyes. But as Gorsch's notes crashed into each other, the cat suddenly opened his eyes. The cat jumped at the closed door, but it wouldn't open. This was really too much for the cat. He was so upset that bright sparks flew from his eyes, nose, and whiskers. The cat started running around like he just couldn't keep still.

Gorsch liked what was happening, so he played even harder.

"Thank you, that's enough, Mr. Gorsch. Thank you!" said the cat. "Please, stop! I promise never to tell you what to do again! And I will never tell you what to play ever again!"

"Quiet!" shouted Gorsch. "We're at the part where they catch the tiger."

All the while, the cat ran around the house, jumping at the walls. He went around and around in circles.

This was making Gorsch feel rather

dizzy. So he said, "All right, I'm done now," and stopped playing.

The cat became quiet again and tried to look as though everything was fine.

"Mr. Gorsch," he said, "your playing is a bit off tonight, isn't it?"

This made Gorsch feel sad and angry again, so he took out a cigarette and a match.

"So what?" he said. "Are you sure *you're* not a bit off tonight? Let's see your tongue."

The cat put out his tongue.

"A-ha! See? It looks a bit rough!" said the cellist. Then he struck his match on the cat's tongue. Then he used the fire to light his cigarette. In his surprise, the cat ran to the door with his tongue still out and hit his head against it. Then he hit his head against the door two more times, trying to run away.

Gorsch just watched for a while. Then, when he'd had enough, he said, "All right, I'll let you out. Just don't come back again!"

Gorsch opened the door and the cat ran outside. Gorsch laughed quietly to himself as he watched the cat run across the field. Then, he lay down in his bed and slept peacefully, as if all his troubles were gone.

The next night, Gorsch came home as usual. He brought his cello in its big, black box. After he had drunk some water, he began to play the cello again. Midnight came and went. Then it was one o'clock, then it was two o'clock. Still, Gorsch continued to play.

Suddenly, Gorsch heard a knock on the ceiling.

"Is that you again, cat?" called out Gorsch. "I told you not to come back!"

But it was not the cat. A bird flew into the house from a little hole in the ceiling. The bird landed on the floor in front of Gorsch. It was a cuckoo.

"Great, now birds are coming in too," said Gorsch. "What do *you* want?"

"I would like to learn music," said the bird.

"How can you learn music? All you can sing is *cuckoo, cuckoo*," said Gorsch.

"You're right," said the bird, "but singing *cuckoo* is difficult and takes great practice."

"Difficult? I'm sure the only difficult thing is having to sing so much all the time. But the notes can't be that hard."

"No, the notes are very hard. See, if I sing like this—*cuckoo*—and then I sing like this—*cuckoo*—the notes are very different."

"They sound the same to me," said Gorsch.

"Your ears are not trained to hear the difference," said the bird. "To us cuckoos, you could sing *cuckoo* ten thousand times and they would all sound different."

"Fine, I believe you," said Gorsch. "But if you're so good, why do you want to learn music from me?"

"I want to learn the scale."

"Why?"

"I have to learn it if I want to go traveling."

"Why do you want to go traveling?"

"Please, Mr. Gorsch, teach me the scale. If you play it for me, I'll sing along," said the bird.

"Fine! I'll play it three times. But when I'm finished, you have to go."

Gorsch sat back down. He took up the cello and played the scale.

Do, re, mi, fa, sol, la, ti, do.

But the bird did not look happy. "That's not right," he said.

"What do you mean? You do it then."

The bird waited a moment, then he sang a single *cuckoo*.

"That's not a scale!" said Gorsch. "If you think that's a scale, then all the notes of the Sixth Symphony must sound the same to you cuckoos!"

"No, they sound very different," said the bird. "And it's also very difficult when you play many notes one after the other."

"Do you mean like this?" said Gorsch. He played many *cuckoos* on the cello one after the other.

This made the bird so happy that he began to sing *cuckoo, cuckoo* together with Gorsch as he played. On and on they went together—*cuckoo, cuckoo*.

Gorsch's hand began to hurt. He stopped playing.

"I think that's enough," he said.

The bird, however, didn't seem to think it was enough. He just continued to sing until he ended with a *cuck—cuck—cuck—cu*.

This made Gorsch angry.

"If you're done now, just get out of here," he said.

"Please, Mr. Gorsch," said the bird.

"Play it one more time. You're not playing it quite right yet."

"What! *You* came here to learn from *me*! I don't need to learn from you. Just get out of here."

"Please, just one more time," said the bird.

"All right," said Gorsch, taking up his cello again. "Just one more time."

"Please play for as long as possible, if you don't mind," said the bird.

"Oh, goodness," said Gorsch. He began to play. The bird got very excited again, singing *cuckoo*, *cuckoo* while he rocked his body from side to side.

At first, Gorsch was angry, but this soon changed. He began to have the strange feeling that it really was the bird who was hitting the right notes. The more

Gorsch the Cellist

he played, the more it seemed to him that the bird was better than him.

"I can't keep going," Gorsch thought. "I'm becoming 'cuckoo' myself!" With this thought, he stopped.

The bird was surprised with the sudden stop. He sang *cuckoo, cuck—cuck—cuck—cu—*and stopped as before.

"Why did you stop?" the bird asked. "Any good cuckoo would keep singing as loud as he could until he just couldn't go on anymore."

"Did you really think I could keep wasting time like this forever?" asked Gorsch. "It's almost morning now! You've got to go."

Gorsch pointed at the window. They could see that the sky was getting lighter.

"Can't we continue until the sun is up

all the way? It will only be a little longer."

"No! You think you can have everything your way! If you don't leave now, I'll just eat you for breakfast!"

Gorsch stamped his foot hard. This made the bird afraid, and he flew straight into the closed window. The bird fell to the ground.

"You stupid bird!" said Gorsch. He quickly went to the window to try to open it. But the window was very old. It took many tries to open it even a little. He was still pushing and pulling at the window when the bird flew into it again. Then Gorsch saw that the bird had hurt his head.

"Just wait a little bit," said Gorsch. "I'm going to open it for you."

After much pushing, Gorsch got the

window open a few inches. But then the bird picked himself up and flew straight into the window again. He flew with all his might, and he hit the window much harder than before. He dropped to the floor and lay still.

Gorsch tried to pick up the bird. He wanted to take him to the door, open it, and let him fly out that way. But the bird jumped up. He looked like he was going to fly at the window again. Surprised and worried, Gorsch kicked the window as hard as he could.

The glass broke and the whole window fell outside into the yard. The bird flew out of the large hole in the wall. He flew and flew into the sky until Gorsch could not see him anymore. Gorsch stayed at the window watching for a while, but he was so tired. Soon, he dropped himself in a corner of the room and slept.

The next night, Gorsch played his cello again late into the night. Then, sometime after midnight, there was a knock at the door.

"I won't waste any more time with any visitors," thought Gorsch. "I'll act mean and angry and drive the visitor away from the beginning."

The door opened a little bit, and a young badger came into his house. Gorsch began to shout.

"Hey, you! Have you ever heard of badger soup?"

The badger just looked at Gorsch and seemed to think for a little while.

"No, I've never heard of it," he said. He sat there looking so serious that

Gorsch wanted to laugh out loud. But he tried to continue looking angry and said, "Well, I'll tell you what it is. I make badger soup by cooking a badger like you with some salt in water. Then I eat it."

The young badger sat and thought some more.

"But my father told me to come and study with you because you're a nice man. He said I shouldn't be afraid of you," the badger said.

Gorsch couldn't help but laugh at this.

"Well, what are you supposed to study?" he said. "I'm very busy, and tired too."

At this the young badger got excited and took a step forward.

"I'm going to play the drum!" he said. "I'm supposed to learn how to play the drum in time with your cello."

"But where is your drum?"

The young badger took out two sticks that he had tied to his back.

"What are those supposed to do?" asked Gorsch.

"I'll show you," said the badger. "Please play 'The Happy Driver.'"

"What is that? I've never heard of it. Is it jazz?"

"Here's the music," said the badger. He handed Gorsch a piece of paper with music on it.

Gorsch looked at it and laughed.

"This is a funny song!" he said. "Well, all right. Let's try it."

Gorsch started playing the cello. As he played, he watched the young badger. He was surprised when he started to play his two sticks on the body of the cello in time. What's more, he was pretty good! Gorsch found himself enjoying playing with the little badger.

When they finished playing 'The Happy Driver,' the little badger was quiet. He seemed to be thinking.

"When you play the second string you fall a little behind," he said. "It throws off the beat."

Gorsch was surprised. What the little badger said was true. Last night, Gorsch had noticed that when he played the second string, it took longer than it should to make a sound.

"I think you're right. This old cello is no good," he said sadly.

The badger looked sad and thought for a little while.

"I wonder if we could figure out what's wrong with it," he said. "Could you please play it again?"

"Sure," said Gorsch. He started to play again. The little badger listened closely. But by the time they finished, the sky was getting light again.

"Oh! It's almost morning," said the badger. "Thank you very much." Then the badger picked up his two sticks and tied them to his back again. Then he hurried out the door.

Gorsch sat still for a little while. He enjoyed the feeling of the cool morning air that came in through the broken window. Then he decided to rest before he went into town again. He lay down in bed and fell asleep.

The next night, Gorsch stayed up late

playing the cello again. He was very tired and it was well past midnight when there was another knock at the door. But by this time Gorsch was used to it.

"Come in," he said.

Into the house came a mouse. Along with her came a baby mouse. He was so small that he was no bigger than your little finger. Gorsch smiled.

The mother mouse put a nut on the floor in front of Gorsch. Then she bowed and said, "Mr. Gorsch, my baby is very sick. I'm afraid he might die. Please, be so kind as to make him well again."

"How am *I* supposed to do that?" asked Gorsch.

"I know you make sick people better every day. You're good at it," answered the mother mouse.

"I don't know what you mean."

"Well, you made the rabbit's grandmother better. And the badger's father too. You even saved that mean old owl. And it's not very nice of you to help all those other people but not help my baby."

"I don't understand!" said Gorsch. "I've never saved an owl or a rabbit. It's true that the young badger was here last night, but I've never even met his father."

The mother mouse started crying.

"Oh, if my baby had just gotten sick sooner! You were playing the cello here all night, shaking the floor with the sound. But as soon as my baby got sick, you stopped. And now you won't play any more. My poor baby!"

"What?" cried Gorsch. "Are you saying that when I play my cello it makes

Gorsch the Cellist

sick animals feel better? But why?"

"Yes, that's right. You see, when the animals around here get sick, they go under your floor to listen."

"And that cures them?"

"Yes, it's very good for the circulation. The animals feel so much better. Sometimes they're cured right away. Sometimes they feel better as soon as they get home."

"I see," said Gorsch. "I think I'm beginning to understand. The sound of my cello shakes the floor. It must act as a kind of massage. All right, then. Let's try it. I'll play for your baby."

Gorsch took his cello and got ready to play. Then he picked up the baby mouse and dropped him into the hole of the cello.

"I'll go in there with him" said the mother, sounding worried. "I know all the hospitals would let me."

But when she tried to climb in through the hole, she found she couldn't fit.

"Are you all right?" she cried into the hole. "Did you fall the right way and land on your four feet, like I always tell you?"

"Yes, I'm all right," said the baby mouse. It was hard to hear his little voice coming from the little hole. "I landed really well."

"Don't worry, he's all right," said Gorsch. "There's no need to cry now."

Gorsch put the mother down on the floor and picked up his bow. Then he began to play. The sound of the cello shook the floor. The mother listened closely for a while, but she still seemed worried. She stopped Gorsch.

"That's enough, thank you," she said.

"Can we take him out now and see if it worked?"

"Oh, is that all it takes?" asked Gorsch. He laid the cello on its side and put his hand to the hole. Soon, the baby mouse climbed out of the hole and onto his hand. Gorsch set him down on the ground. The baby had his eyes closed and his whole body shook and shook.

"Are you all right? Do you feel better?" asked the mother mouse.

The baby kept his eyes closed and shook some more. Then, suddenly, he jumped into the air. He ran around in circles happily.

"Oh! He's feeling better! Thank you, Mr. Gorsch! Thank you so much." The mother mouse joined her baby and ran a few circles with him. Then, she bowed over and over to Gorsch. "Thank you, thank you," she said about ten times.

For some reason, Gorsch felt rather sorry for the little mice.

"Do you like bread?" he asked.

"Oh! We've heard it's very nice, but we've never tried it. Of course, we never come into your kitchen. And we would never steal any from you after all that you have done for us."

"No, I don't mean that!" said Gorsch. "I just thought you might like to eat some. Wait a minute. I'll give some to your baby. It will be good for his health."

Gorsch went to his kitchen and got some bread. He tore off a piece and put it in front of them.

The mother mouse began to laugh and cry at the same time. She bowed again to Gorsch. Then, being very careful, she took the bread in her mouth and carried it out of the house as her baby led the way.

"My goodness," said Gorsch. "Mice are very tiring to talk to!"

He lay down on his bed and fell fast asleep.

On the day of the Sixth Symphony performance, Gorsch played hard with the Venus Orchestra. When they had finished, all the musicians carried their instruments off the stage. They listened as the audience clapped and clapped. Most people had even stood up. The clapping wouldn't end.

The theater manager came behind the curtain. "They want an encore!" he said. "Can you play a little something for them?"

"No," said the conductor. "There's nothing we can play well enough to follow such an important work."

"Well, can't you at least go and say something to them then?"

"No," said the conductor again. Then suddenly he turned to Gorsch. "Go out there and play something."

"Me?" cried Gorsch in shock.

"Yes, you!" agreed the theater manager.

"Yes. Go ahead, Gorsch," said the conductor.

The other musicians handed Gorsch his cello. Then they pushed him through the curtains, onto the stage. Gorsch stood alone, holding his cello. Still, everybody continued to clap. Some were clapping louder now. It even sounded like some were cheering for Gorsch.

"They're making fun of me!" thought Gorsch. "Well, I'll fix that. I'll play them 'Tiger Hunt in India.'"

With that thought, he walked to the middle of the stage. He sat down and put his bow to the cello. Then he began to play.

Gorsch played with all the energy of an angry elephant, just as he did the day the cat came to visit. The audience went quiet and listened closely. Gorsch went on. He came to the part where sparks had flown out of the cat's eyes. Then he came to the part where the cat ran straight into the door. On he played with great energy.

When Gorsch was finished, he stood up and walked off the stage. He did not look at the audience. He did not say a single word. He went straight into the musician's room. There, he saw the conductor and the musicians sitting with their mouths open. But Gorsch did not care anymore what people thought of him. So he walked straight to a chair and sat down.

"There is something strange about this evening," Gorsch thought.

The conductor stood up.

"Gorsch! You were wonderful!" he said. "The music was not a great work, but you kept us listening! You've become so much better in the last week! Why, I would say that ten days ago, you played like a new musician. Now, you play like a master! I always knew you could do it if you just tried hard enough!"

All the others joined in. "Well done,

Gorsch the Cellist

Gorsch!" they said.

Gorsch heard the conductor explaining to someone. "You see, Gorsch can do such a thing because he's strong. To do what he did would have killed most other men."

Gorsch went home much later that night.

First, he drank a glass of water. Then, he opened the window. Looking into the sky where the cuckoo had flown, he said, "I'm sorry, cuckoo. I wasn't really angry with you!"

The Police Chief

水の豊かなプハラの町には、毒もみをして魚を取ってはならないという法律がある。毒をいれた袋を水につけてもみ、浮いてきた魚をとるのが毒もみ漁法である。ある夏、新しい警察署長がプハラの町に着任する。ちょうどそのころ、川で誰かが毒もみをしている形跡がよく見られるようになり、警察は捜査を始める。しかし半年が過ぎても犯人は捕まらず……。

読みはじめる前に

The Police Chief に出てくる語です。あらかじめ確認しておきましょう。

- ☐ police chief 警察署長
- ☐ catfish ナマズ
- ☐ barber 理髪師
- ☐ lie うそをつく
- ☐ no matter how どんなに〜であろうとも
- ☐ poison bag 毒の入った袋
- ☐ bark 木の皮
- ☐ Day of the Horse 午の日《5日のこと。中国語で「午」は「五」と同じ発音（wǔ）であることから》
- ☐ belly 腹
- ☐ small pox 天然痘
- ☐ fine 細かい
- ☐ oak オーク《ブナ科の樹木の総称》
- ☐ eel ウナギ
- ☐ mayor 町長
- ☐ arrest 逮捕する
- ☐ criminal 犯罪者
- ☐ detective 探偵
- ☐ trial 裁判
- ☐ (be) sentenced to death 死刑判決を受ける
- ☐ (be) moved 感銘する

Four great rivers with water as cold as ice ran down Karakon Mountain. The rivers met in the town of Puhara. As they came together, they made one wide river. Here, in this large river, the peaceful waters were very still and clear. You could see the clouds and the trees in the water.

During the heavy rains, the river would rise. Then the low land around the river would also fill with water. It formed little lakes that were full of fish. Some of the lakes were there all year.

There were many catfish in the little lakes. But the people of Puhara did not like to eat catfish. So, the fish continued to increase in number.

One year, the barber named Richiki said that a great big fish had come to live in one of the lakes. Richiki said it had swum there from the ocean. Most of the adults and some of the older children smiled at this. They knew it couldn't possibly be true. Richiki was known for being a terrible barber, and he often lied. But the younger children still went to the lakes to see the great big fish from the sea. No matter how long they looked, though, they never saw any sign of the big fish. Most people stopped listening to Richiki at all.

There is a law in Puhara that says, "You must not use guns to kill birds, and you must not use poison bags to catch

The Police Chief

fish." Richiki the barber says this is how you make and use the poison bags:

"First, take some *sansho* bark on a very dark night. It must be on the Day of the Horse in spring. Dry the bark twice in the hot sun. Then, make it into powder. Put this into a bag together with burned wood. The wood must come from the maple tree, and it must be burned on a fine, sunny day. Then put this bag into the water."

When this is done, the fish drink the poison and die. They come to the top of the water with their white bellies up.

One of the most important jobs of the Puhara police was to stop people from catching fish with these poison bags.

Then, one summer, a new police chief came to the town of Puhara. He wore a long, red coat that had beautiful gold buttons. He went out every day to keep a careful watch over the town.

If he saw a horse that looked tired, he would ask the owner if the horse's bags were too heavy. If a baby cried loudly, he would tell the mother it was small pox.

Around the same time, there were some people who began to break the law of Puhara. The fish disappeared from some of the lakes along the river. Sometimes there were dead fish at the top of the water. Often, after a Day of the Horse in spring, people would find the bark missing from the *sansho* tree. But the chief and his policemen didn't seem to think that such things were really happening.

But, one morning, a group of children

discovered something when they began to talk.

"The police chief got so angry at me the other day," one of the children said.

"Wow! The chief himself?"

"Yes! I threw a stone by the lake. I didn't know anybody was there. But the chief and three or four men were hiding by the pond. They were trying to catch the people who catch fish with the poison bags."

"What did the chief say to you?"

"He said, 'Who threw a stone? We're busy here, trying to catch people who are breaking the law! Go away and don't tell anyone what you saw here.'"

"Then I'm sure the person with the poison bags will be caught soon," said another child.

The Police Chief

But six months passed and still nobody was caught. The children of Puhara began talking again.

"Listen to this!" said one child. "Last night, just as the moon came up, I saw the police chief all dressed in black. He was talking to that man who goes hunting with a gun. The police chief said to him, 'I want this wood powder finer next time!' The man said something back. Then the police chief said, 'You want me to pay two dollars for this? I know you mix oak wood into it! Dream on!' I'm sure they were talking about powdered *sansho* bark and burned wood!"

Hearing this, another child shouted, "Oh, I remember something! Once, the chief bought two bags of burned wood at our house! It's used with the bark to make the poison!"

"Yes! That's it!" cried the other children.

When Richiki the barber heard about this, he started to add up some numbers. He didn't have many customers and lots of free time, so he could do this. He wrote down:

Cost of Poison-Bag Fishing:
- One bag of bark — 2 dollars
- One bag of burned wood — 30 coins
- Total — 2 dollars, 30 coins

Money Made from Poison-Bag Fishing:
- Thirteen eels — 13 dollars
- Other fish (estimated) — 10 dollars
- Total — 23 dollars

Police Chief's Profit: 20 dollars, 70 coins

The Police Chief

The talk spread all around town. It got so bad that when the children saw any policeman, they would act like they were afraid and run away. Then they would stop, turn, and yell, "Hey, poison-bag policeman! Why don't you leave us the catfish at least?"

It got so bad that the mayor of Puhara stepped in. He took six of the town's leaders with him and went to talk to the police chief.

As they sat in the chief's room, the chief seemed to be looking somewhere far away.

"Do you know what the people in town are saying? They say that someone continues to break the poison-bag fishing law. What are your thoughts on this?"

"Do you think it's true?" asked the police chief.

"I'm afraid so," said the mayor. "The *sansho* trees around my house are all missing their bark. And the people say that dead fish are often found in the water."

The police chief gave a strange little smile at this.

"Oh, that's what the people are saying, is it?"

"Yes, it is," said the mayor, feeling rather uneasy. "In fact, the children are saying... well, they're saying that *you* are the poison bag man. It's so strange, isn't it?"

At these words, the police chief jumped up from his chair.

"It's awful!" he said. "It shows that I am not doing my job! I will arrest the criminal right now."

The Police Chief

"Well, do you have any idea who it is?"

"Let me see. Yes, I do. In fact, I know perfectly well."

"Who is it then?"

"*I* am the poison bag man!"

"You! So it was you all along?" said the shocked mayor.

"Yes."

"You're sure?"

"Of course."

With this, the police chief called for the head detective.

Then the police chief was tied up and put on trial. He was sentenced to death.

Just before the big sword cut his head off, the police chief smiled. Then he said:

"It was fun! If it were up to me, I would do nothing but catch fish with poison bags all day long! And now, I'll go do it in hell."

All the people were very moved.

The Restaurant of Many Orders

森の奥で狩りをして
いた２人の紳士は、道案内と
はぐれ、帰り道が分からなくなっ
てしまう。寒くて空腹でくたびれた
２人の前に、山奥には不似合いな建て
構えの立派なレストランが現れる。不
思議に思いながらも店に入ると、「注文
の多い料理店ですがお気になさらない
でください」という注意書きがある。
注文が殺到する人気店なのだと、
２人は期待に胸を膨らませ
るが……。

読みはじめる前に

The Restaurant of Many Orders に出てくる語です。あらかじめ確認しておきましょう。

- [ ] order　　　　　　注文
- [ ] dizzy　　　　　　めまいがする
- [ ] bark　　　　　　吠える
- [ ] cost　　　　　　（金、費用が）かかる
- [ ] inn　　　　　　　宿屋
- [ ] wild cat　　　　　ヤマネコ
- [ ] enter　　　　　　入る
- [ ] joy　　　　　　　喜び
- [ ] mud　　　　　　泥
- [ ] purse　　　　　　財布
- [ ] pointed　　　　　先のとがった
- [ ] electricity　　　　電気
- [ ] bowl　　　　　　ボウル、鉢
- [ ] chapped　　　　　（肌が）荒れた
- [ ] pour　　　　　　注ぐ、浴びせる
- [ ] vinegar　　　　　酢
- [ ] poor thing　　　　気の毒な人
- [ ] crumple　　　　　しわくちゃになる
- [ ] waste paper　　　古紙
- [ ] growl　　　　　　（～に向かって）うなる
- [ ] straw cape　　　　みの《わら製の雨具》

Two young gentlemen were walking deep in the forest. They were dressed like British soldiers. They had new guns at their side, and two big white dogs followed at their feet. The two men talked as they went.

"You know, the country around here is awful," one said. "There are no birds or animals anywhere! I would love to shoot at something right now. Bang, bang! I'd shoot at anything, as long as it moves."

"I agree," said the other. "It would be so fun to kill a deer right now. I can just see him running in circles then falling down on the ground."

The men were *very* deep in the mountains. They were so deep, in fact, that the experienced hunter who had come as their guide had walked away and disappeared somewhere. What's more, the forest was so dark and dangerous that both dogs were afraid. They both got dizzy, barked for a while, then died.

"That dog cost me two thousand and four hundred dollars!"

"Mine cost two thousand and eight hundred," said the other man.

The first gentleman started to look worried.

"I should probably go head back now," he said.

"You know, I was just thinking the same thing," said the other. "I'm feeling a little cold and hungry. I'll join you."

"All right," said the first. "Let's go back to the inn we stayed at yesterday. We can buy a few chickens to eat there."

"Yes, that's a good idea. Let's go home then."

But the trouble was they didn't know how to go back.

Suddenly, it got very windy. The trees moved back and forth. The leaves shook, making strange noises. It got very cold.

"I really am hungry!" one gentleman said. "I haven't eaten anything all day long!"

"Me too," said the other. "I don't feel like walking any more."

"Oh, I wish I had something to eat!"

The forest and the wind made strange noises all around them as they talked.

Just then, one gentleman happened to

look up. And there, standing in front of them, was a fine building. A sign over the door said, "Restaurant Wild Cat House."

"Look at this!" he said. "It's perfect! This forest isn't so wild after all. Let's go in."

"It's strange that a building like this is here in the middle of the forest, isn't it? But I guess we shall be able to eat something there."

"Of course!" said the other. "It says 'restaurant' on the sign!"

"Well, let's give it a try. I feel like I could die of hunger."

They walked through the door and into the front room. It was very beautiful inside, with white walls everywhere. There was a glass door just ahead. Over it was another sign. It read, "Please come

in. Feel free to help yourself. There's no need to wait."

This made the two gentlemen very happy.

"Look at that!" said one of them. "You see? Things always work out well in the end. All day we've been having bad luck. But look at how lucky we are now! That sign says that we don't even have to pay!"

"It does seem to be saying that," said the other. "I think that's what 'feel free to help yourself' means."

They pushed the door open and walked in. They entered a long hall. They found another sign on the back of the door. It said, "Guests who are young or fat are especially welcome."

This filled both men with joy.

"Look! It says we are especially welcome!"

"Yes! Because we are both young and rather fat!"

They walked quickly down the long hall. Soon, they came to another door. It was painted bright blue.

"What a strange place!" said one of the young, fat gentleman. "Why are there so many doors?"

"Well, it's because this is the Russian way," said the other young, fat gentleman. "They always use many doors in places that are cold or in the mountains."

They were just opening the blue door when they saw another sign above it. In large, yellow letters, it read, "We hope you will like this restaurant of many orders."

"I suppose many people like this place," said one. "It's quite interesting that a place all the way in the forest is so popular."

"Of course! Even in the city, none of the best restaurants are on the main streets."

They soon came to another door. They opened it and walked through. On the other side, a sign said, "There really are so many orders. We hope you won't mind."

"Now what do you think that means?" one asked.

"Hmm. I think it means they're busy. They must have a lot of orders coming in. It will take a long time before the food comes out. Or something like that."

"Yes, I guess you're right. But I do

want to sit down and eat as soon as possible, don't you?"

"Yes. I'm so hungry!"

But the young men found there was yet another door. Next to it was a mirror hanging on the wall. There was a brush lying beneath the mirror. A sign in red letters said, "Guests are asked to please brush their hair and get the mud off of their shoes here."

"What a clean and fine restaurant this is!"

"They must want things just right. I think some of their guests must be very rich."

The two young men brushed their hair and cleaned the mud off of their boots.

But when they put the brush back, a strange thing happened. The brush disappeared, and a strong wind blew through the room. Suddenly afraid, the two gentlemen held onto each other and ran through the next door. Both men felt that if they didn't eat something soon, almost anything could happen.

In the next room was another sign. It read, "Please leave your guns here."

"Well, said one young gentleman, "no one eats with their gun, right?"

"Right," said the other. "I'm starting to think that all the guests at this restaurant must be important people. There are so many rules to follow here."

They put down their guns. There was another door. This one was black, and it said, "Please take off your hats, coats, and shoes."

"What do you think? Should we take

them off?"

"I think so. These guests must be *really* important. We don't want to be the only ones not following the rules."

They took off their hats, coats, and shoes. They went through the next door. On the other side was a sign that read, "Please take off your tie pins, glasses, purses, and anything else with metal in it, especially anything pointed."

Next to the door stood a safe. It was big and black, and it had a strong lock on it.

"Of course! They must use electricity while they're cooking. So bringing in metal must be dangerous. That's what I think it means."

"I guess you're right."

So the two young, fat gentlemen took

off their coats, glasses, tie pins, and everything else that was metal or pointed. They put everything in the safe and locked it.

They continued on their way. The next door they came across had a glass bowl in front of it. It had some cream in it. The sign on the door said, "Please spread cream from the bowl all over your face. Put some on your hands and feet too."

"Now, why would they want us to put cream on?"

"Well, if it's very cold outside and too warm inside, your skin gets chapped. This will help. You know, they must get only the very best and most important people coming here. I think we might end up meeting royal people!"

The gentlemen put the cream on their

faces. Then they spread it on their hands. They took off their socks and spread it on their feet as well. There was still a little left in the bowl, so they ate it, acting like they were just putting more on their faces.

In a hurry, they opened the next door. But they found another sign. It said, "Did you put on enough cream? On your ears too?" A smaller bowl of cream sat there.

"Oh, I forgot about my ears!" said one. "I don't want them getting chapped either. The owner of this restaurant really thinks of everything."

"Yes, he really does. But you know, I wouldn't mind eating something now. I wonder how many more rooms we have left to go through?"

But the next sign read, "The meal will be ready soon. Really, it should only take another fifteen minutes. But for now, please pour this perfume over your head."

Sitting in front of the door was a beautiful bottle.

But when the two gentlemen poured it on themselves, they noticed something strange. The perfume smelled a lot like vinegar.

"Oh, this stuff doesn't smell right," said one. "What do you think is wrong with it?"

"It must be a mistake," said the other. "One of the helpers must have had a cold and put the wrong thing in the bottle."

When they opened the door and went through, they saw another sign. In big letters, it said, "You poor things must be tired of all these orders. But we promise this is the last one. Please put some salt all

The Restaurant of Many Orders

over yourself."

A blue pot full of salt sat there. This time, both young men were suddenly very afraid. They looked at each others' cream-covered faces.

"I don't like this," said one.

"Me neither," said the other.

"I think 'lots of orders' means that *they* are giving *us* orders!"

"Yes! And I'm starting to think that 'restaurant' doesn't mean a place where we eat food, but a place where w-w-we…"

He began to shake in fear. He shook so hard that he couldn't continue.

"You mean where w-w-we are e-e-eaten? Oh, dear!" said the other. He, too, began to shake. He shook so hard that he couldn't continue either.

"Let's run!" Still shaking, one of the

gentlemen turned and pushed the door behind him. But it would not open.

At the other end of the room was another door. It was stranger than the other doors. It had two big keyholes in it. The door was made of wood and it had a large knife and fork painted on it. Next to it was a sign that read, "It is so nice of you to come here. You've done very well. Now just come inside, please."

But the most terrible thing was this: there were two blue eyes that were watching them through the keyhole.

"Oh, dear!" cried one of the gentlemen.

"Oh, *dear*!" cried the other.

They both started crying.

Then they heard voices talking quietly on the other side of the door.

"Oh, no. They know now," one voice said.

"Well, what did you think would happen?" the other voice said. "It's because of the way the master wrote those signs. He wrote 'you poor things,' and all that. It was no good!"

"Well, either way we won't get to eat anything. Not even their bones."

"You're right. But if they won't hurry and come in here, the master will be so angry at us!"

"Shall we call to them? Yes, that's what we should do. Hello! Hello, gentlemen! Come this way, quickly! The dishes are clean and the vegetables are salted. All we need to do now is put you onto the dishes! This way now!"

The two young gentlemen were so

afraid that their faces were crumpled like pieces of waste paper. They looked at each other and shook and cried.

The voices on the other side of the door laughed. Then a voice shouted again, "This way! Come this way! If you cry like that, all the cream will wash off!"

Then he seemed to say to someone else, "Yes, sir. They're coming soon, sir."

Now, the voice shouted again at the two young gentlemen. "Come on, we're in a hurry!"

"Yes, hurry up! The master has his knife and fork ready. He's waiting just for you!"

But the two young gentlemen just cried and cried and cried.

Then, suddenly, they heard a loud noise. It was the barking of dogs! Behind them, two big white dogs came running into the room. The eyes behind the keyholes disappeared. The dogs ran around and around, barking and growling. They jumped at the door. The door flew open, and the dogs disappeared as they ran into the darkness beyond. From the darkness came the sound of an angry cat meowing and hissing.

Then the room disappeared. The two young gentlemen found themselves standing in the forest. They were shaking and cold. Their coats, shoes, guns, and all their other things were on the ground around them. A strong wind shook the leaves and the trees.

The dogs came running back and someone behind them called out, "Gentlemen! Gentlemen!"

"We're here, we're here! This way!" they called back.

The experienced hunter came toward them through the forest. His straw cape blew in the wind. The two young gentlemen felt safe at last.

They ate the food the guide had brought with him. Then they returned to the city. They bought some chickens to eat on the way.

But even when they were back at home in the city, no matter how many hot baths they took, their faces were all crumpled like waste paper. And they were never the same again.

The Wild Cat and the Acorns

　ある日、一郎は不思議な手紙を受け取る。裁判の判事として出廷を求めるという内容で、差し出し主は山猫とある。一郎は大喜びででかけていく。木々や滝や、きのこの楽団たちに道を教えてもらいながら、やっと山猫のもとにたどり着くと、そこでは一面のどんぐりたちが、判決を求めてどなりあっていた……。

読みはじめる前に

The Wild Cat and the Acorns に出てくる語です。
あらかじめ確認しておきましょう。

- [ ] acorn　　　　　　　　ドングリ
- [ ] case　　　　　　　　　事件
- [ ] nut　　　　　　　　　 木の実
- [ ] wagon　　　　　　　　荷馬車
- [ ] Flute Falls　　　　　　 笛ふきの滝
- [ ] whistle　　　　　　　　(口)笛を吹く
- [ ] squirrel　　　　　　　　リス
- [ ] path　　　　　　　　　小道
- [ ] roll around　　　　　　 転げまわる
- [ ] spade　　　　　　　　 鋤
- [ ] fifth-grader　　　　　　 五年生
- [ ] cheer up　　　　　　　元気になる
- [ ] whiskers　　　　　　　ほおひげ
- [ ] comfortable　　　　　　快適な、心地よい
- [ ] badly　　　　　　　　　とても、ひどく
- [ ] crackle　　　　　　　　(火が)パチパチ音を立てる
- [ ] robe　　　　　　　　　(裁判官などの)法服、ローブ
- [ ] good-for-nothing　　　　役立たずな
- [ ] preacher　　　　　　　説教師
- [ ] least　　　　　　　　　最も少ない
- [ ] esquire　　　　　　　　～殿
- [ ] wording　　　　　　　　言い回し
- [ ] pint　　　　　　　　　パイント《0.47ℓ》

One Saturday night, Ichiro received a very strange letter. It said:

> September 19
>
> Mr. Ichiro Kaneta:
>
> Pleased to know as how you are. I have a hard case to judge tomorrow. So please come. Please, no bringing guns.
>
> Yours truly,
> Wild Cat

There was nothing else. The writing was terrible. The ink was so thick and wet in places that it got on Ichiro's fingers. But Ichiro was very excited. When no one was looking, he put the letter in his bag to take it to school. He jumped up and down with joy all over the house.

Even as he lay in bed at night, he couldn't stop thinking about Wild Cat. He was so excited that he didn't fall asleep until very late.

When he woke up the next morning,

The Wild Cat and the Acorns

he went outside. The hills, clean and fresh in the morning sun, rose up to the blue sky. Ichiro ate his breakfast quickly. Then he went alone up the path that ran along the river. A strong wind shook the trees. Their nuts fell onto the ground.

"Hello, nut trees," Ichiro called. "Did Wild Cat come this way?"

The trees stopped shaking for a moment and replied.

"Wild Cat? Yes, he came through here in a wagon early in the morning. He was going east."

"East? That's where I'm headed! I'll keep going this way and see. Thank you, nut trees!"

But the trees didn't answer. They just kept throwing their nuts on the ground.

Ichiro continued on his way. He soon

came across Flute Falls. At Flute Falls, there was a snow-white wall of rock. In the middle of it was a small hole. Clear water ran out of it, making a whistling sound like a flute. Ichiro shouted up at the falls:

"Hello, Flute Falls! Did Wild Cat come this way?"

"Wild Cat?" Flute Falls said in its high, whistle-like voice. "Yes, he hurried by here in a wagon earlier. He was going west."

"West?" asked Ichiro. "That's where my house is. How strange! Well, I'll go a little farther and see. Thank you, Flute Falls."

But Flute Falls did not answer. It was already busy whistling again. So Ichiro continued on. Soon, he came to

The Wild Cat and the Acorns

a tree. Under the tree, a group of white mushrooms were playing together in a mushroom orchestra. *Tiddly-tum-tum, tiddly-ta-ta.* Ichiro got down close to the ground.

"Hello, Mushrooms," he said. "Did Wild Cat come this way?"

"Wild cat? Yes, he came by here in a wagon early this morning. He was going south."

"How strange," said Ichiro again. "South heads to those mountains there. Well, I guess I'll go a bit farther and see. Thank you, Mushrooms."

But the mushrooms didn't answer. They were already busy again, playing their strange music. *Tiddly-tum-tum, tiddly-ta-ta.*

Ichiro kept walking, and soon he

noticed a squirrel jumping between trees.

"Hello, Squirrel!" called Ichiro. "Did you see Wild Cat come this way?"

"Wild Cat?" said the squirrel. He held his hand over his eyes to block the sun. "Yes, he went past here in a great hurry when it was still dark this morning. He was in a wagon going south."

"South?" said Ichiro. "That's the second time I've been told that. Well, I'll go a little farther and see. Thank you, Squirrel."

But the squirrel had already left. He jumped between the trees until all Ichiro could see were moving leaves at the top of the tree.

Ichiro continued walking. The path that ran along the river became smaller. Then, farther on, it disappeared. But

The Wild Cat and the Acorns

Ichiro saw another path that led toward the dark forest south of the river. Ichiro headed down this path.

As he walked, the trees came so close together that he could not see the sky above. The path began to climb a hill. Up and up it went. Ichiro's face turned bright red. He was getting very tired. But then, suddenly, he came out into the light. He had arrived at a beautiful field. The grass moved in the wind. All around the field stood fine, tall trees.

There, in the middle of the field, stood a very strange little man. He was watching Ichiro. Slowly, Ichiro walked nearer, but he stopped in surprise. The little man had one white eye that he could not see out of. The white eye rolled around and around, always moving. He wore a kind of worker's coat that Ichiro had never seen before. But the strangest thing of all was that his feet were shaped like spades.

"Excuse me," said Ichiro, "but would you happen to know Wild Cat?"

The little man looked at Ichiro with his one good eye. His mouth turned up into a smile.

"Mr. Wild Cat will be back soon," he said. "I guess you must be Ichiro?"

"That's right," said Ichiro, very surprised. "How did you know?"

The strange little man's smile grew bigger.

"Then you received the letter?"

"Yes. That's why I came here," said Ichiro.

"The letter wasn't well written, was it?" said the strange little man sadly. He

The Wild Cat and the Acorns

looked so sad that Ichiro felt sorry for him.

"No," Ichiro said. "It seemed very good to me."

"What did you think of the handwriting?"

Ichiro couldn't help but smile.

"I thought it was fine. I don't think even a fifth-grader could have written that well."

Suddenly the little man looked sad again.

"By 'fifth-grader,' you probably mean somebody at primary school," he said.

"Oh, no!" said Ichiro. "I mean at university."

The strange little man cheered up. He smiled his biggest smile yet so that his mouth seemed too big for his face.

"*I* wrote that letter!" he shouted happily.

"And who are you?" asked Ichiro.

"I am Mr. Wild Cat's driver!" he answered.

Suddenly, a strong wind blew across the field. The driver gave a deep bow to someone. Surprised, Ichiro turned around and he saw Wild Cat standing behind him.

Wild Cat wore a fine yellow coat. He had a round belly and his two green eyes were perfect circles. He looked at Ichiro as he gave a little bow.

"Good morning," said Ichiro. He bowed in return. "Thank you for your letter."

"Good morning," said Wild Cat. He pulled at his whiskers. "I'm happy to see you. You see, a very difficult case came

The Wild Cat and the Acorns

up the day before yesterday. It's giving me lots of trouble. I don't know what to do about it, so I thought I should ask you. Please, make yourself comfortable. The acorns should be here soon. You know, this trial gives me trouble every year."

He took a cigarette case out from his yellow coat.

"Would you like one?" he asked, offering Ichiro a cigarette.

Ichiro shook his head in surprise.

"No, thank you," he said.

"Oh! That's right. You're still too young," said Wild Cat. He laughed a wise little laugh. Then he lit a match and began to smoke. His driver was standing by and waiting for orders. He seemed to want a cigarette very badly, because big tears were rolling down his face.

Just then, Ichiro heard noises at his feet. It was a crackling kind of sound, like salt being thrown onto a fire. He looked down and saw little, round, gold things all over the ground. When he looked closer, he saw that they were acorns. There must have been more than three hundred of them. They all wore red pants and they were all shouting at each other in their little voices.

"Here they come," said Wild Cat. He threw away his cigarette. In a bit of a hurry, he gave orders to the driver. "You!" he said. "Ring the bell! And cut the grass here, where it's sunny."

The driver did as he was told. He picked up his knife and cut down the grass in front of Wild Cat. The acorns all came running into the area with the

cut grass. They were all still talking and shouting at each other.

Then the driver rang the bell. *Clang, clang!* The bell sounded through the woods. Suddenly, the acorns became quiet. Ichiro noticed that Wild Cat had put on a long black robe. He was now sitting in front of them, looking very important. Ichiro was reminded of a picture he had seen of people all gathered before a large Buddha statue.

"I'd like to remind you," said Wild Cat, "that this is the third day that this case has been going on. Now, why don't you all stop fighting and make up with each other?"

Wild Cat seemed a little nervous but he did a good job making himself sound important. But as soon as he was

The Wild Cat and the Acorns

done speaking, the acorns started talking again.

"No! It's impossible! Whatever you may say, the best acorn is the one with the most pointed head. And I've got the most pointed head."

"No, you're wrong. The roundest acorn is best. I'm the roundest!"

"No, you're both wrong! It's size! The biggest acorn is best. I'm the biggest, so I'm the best!"

"That's wrong too! It's the one who's tallest. I'm the tallest, I tell you!"

"No, it's the one who's best at pushing and pulling! That's me!"

The acorns were talking all at the same time and making such a lot of noise that you had no idea what it was all about.

"That's enough!" yelled Wild Cat. "Where do you think you are? Quiet! Quiet!"

The acorns quieted down again.

"I'm going to remind you again. This is the third day this trial has been going on," said Wild Cat. He pulled at his whiskers until they stood out straight to the side. "Why don't you stop fighting and make up with each other?"

"No, we can't, because the one with the most pointed head is the best!"

"No, the roundest is the best!"

"No, you're wrong! It's the biggest!"

They all began talking again until you had no idea what it was all about.

"That's enough! Where do you think you are?" cried out Wild Cat. "Quiet! Quiet!"

The Wild Cat and the Acorns

Wild Cat pulled at his whiskers, then started again.

"I should not have to remind you that this is the third day this case has been going on. Why don't you stop fighting and be friends again?"

"No, no! Impossible! The one with the most pointed head…"

The acorns began talking and shouting again.

"That's enough!" yelled Wild Cat. "Where do you think you are? Quiet! Quiet!"

"You see the problem?" said Wild Cat to Ichiro quietly. "What should I do?"

Ichiro smiled.

"Here's an idea," he said. "Why don't you tell them the best one is the one who is the most stupid and the most good-for-nothing? I heard a preacher say that once."

Wild Cat agreed to give it a try. He spoke to the acorns in his most important voice.

"Be quiet!" he yelled. "Listen closely. This is my answer to you. The best acorn is the one who is the least important, the most stupid, and the most good-for-nothing!"

The acorns were so quiet you could hear a pin drop.

Wild Cat took off his black robe. He wiped his head and shook Ichiro's hand.

"Thank you very much," Wild Cat said to Ichiro. "You have helped me very much! You ended this difficult case in just a little more than a minute! I hope you will come back as a special judge in my court again. If I send you more letters in

The Wild Cat and the Acorns

the future, you will come, won't you? I'll make sure you are paid every time."

"Yes, of course I'll come. But you don't have to pay me," said Ichiro.

"Oh, but you must take some payment," said Wild Cat. "It's a matter of honor for me. And, from now on, we shall write our letters to 'Ichiro Kaneta, Esquire.' And we shall call this 'the court.' Will that be all right?"

"That would be fine," said Ichiro.

For a moment, Wild Cat was quiet. He pulled at his whiskers as if he were deep in thought. Then, he seemed to make up his mind to say something. He said, "About the wording on the letter—should we write, 'Because of very special business, we kindly ask for your presence at court.'"

Ichiro smiled again.

"Somehow, it sounds a bit funny to me. Maybe you'd better leave that part out."

Wild Cat looked sadly at the ground. He pulled at his whiskers as though he wished he had come up with better words. At last, he said, "Well then, we'll leave it as it is. Now, for your payment today. Would you rather have a pint of gold acorns or a salted fish head?"

"The acorns, please," said Ichiro.

Wild Cat turned to the driver. He seemed glad that Ichiro hadn't chosen the fish head. "Get a pint of gold acorns," he said. "And be quick!"

The driver picked up the acorns from the ground and put them into a square box. When he had filled up the box, he

The Wild Cat and the Acorns

shouted, "One pint of acorns!"

"Right!" said Wild Cat. "Now hurry and get the wagon ready."

Suddenly, a wagon made out of a great white mushroom stood in front of them. Pulling it was a very strange gray horse. In fact, it looked just like a mouse.

"Now we'll take you home," Wild Cat said to Ichiro.

When they got into the wagon, the driver put the box of acorns in next to them. Then they took off down the road. They left the field far behind them. The trees moved out of their way. Ichiro looked at his gold acorns. Wild Cat looked somewhere far away.

But, as the wagon moved, the acorns lost their gold color. Soon, the wagon stopped in front of Ichiro's house. Wild

Cat, the driver, and the mushroom wagon all disappeared into thin air. Ichiro was left standing in front of his home. And the box in his hand held just plain, brown acorns.

From then on, Ichiro did not receive any more letters signed, "Yours truly, Wild Cat." Ichiro still thinks about it from time to time. Maybe he should have let Wild Cat write "we kindly ask for your presence at court" after all?

Word List

- LEVEL 1、2は本文で使われている全ての語を掲載しています。
  LEVEL 3以上は、中学校レベルの語を含みません。ただし、本文で特殊な意味で使われている場合、その意味のみを掲載しています。
- 語形が規則変化する語の見出しは原形で示しています。不規則変化語は本文中で使われている形になっています。
- 一般的な意味を紹介していますので、一部の語で本文で実際に使われている品詞や意味と合っていないことがあります。
- 品詞は以下のように示しています。

名 名詞	代 代名詞	形 形容詞	副 副詞	動 動詞	助動 助動詞
前 前置詞	接 接続詞	間 間投詞	冠 冠詞	略 略語	俗 俗語
熟 熟語	接頭 接頭語	尾 接尾語	記 記号	関代 関係代名詞	

A

- □ **a** 冠 ①1つの, 1人の, ある ②~につき
- □ **able** 形 《be - to ~》(人が)~することができる
- □ **about** 副 ①およそ, 約 ②まわりに, あたりを 前 ①~について ②~のまわりに[の] How about ~? はどうですか。
- □ **above** 前 ~の上に 副 上に
- □ **acorn** 名 ドングリ
- □ **across** 前 ①~を渡って, ~の向こう側に 副 渡って, 向こう側に come across ~に出くわす, ~に遭遇する run across 走って渡る
- □ **act** 動 行動する, 演じる
- □ **add up** ~を合計する
- □ **adult** 名 大人
- □ **afraid** 形 ①心配して ②恐れて, こわがって I'm afraid (that) 残念ながら、悪いけれど~、おそらく be afraid of ~を恐れる, ~を怖がる
- □ **after** 前 ①~の後に[で], ~の次に ②《前後に名詞がきて》次々に~, 何度も~《反復・継続を表す》 副 後に[で] 接 (~した)後に[で] after all やはり, 結局, 何しろ~なのだから one after the other 次々に, 順々に

- □ **afternoon** 名 午後
- □ **again** 副 再び, もう一度 ever again 二度と over and over again 何度も繰り返して
- □ **against** 前 ~に対して, ~にぶつかって
- □ **ago** 副 ~前に
- □ **agree** 動 同意する, 意見が一致する
- □ **a-ha** 間 ははあ, へえ
- □ **ahead** 副 前方に go ahead さあ~しなさい
- □ **air** 名 ①《the -》空中, 空間 ②空気, 《the -》大気 disappear into thin air 虚空に消える jump into the air 空中に飛び上がる
- □ **all** 形 すべての, ~中 代 全部, すべて(のもの[人]) 名 全体 副 まったく, すっかり after all やはり, 結局, 何しろ~なのだから all at once 突然, 出し抜けに all along 初めからずっと all day 一日中 all day long 一日中 all over ~中で, 全体にわたって, ~の至る所で all right 大丈夫で, よろしい, わかった, 承知した all the time ずっと, いつも all the way 最後まで all the while その間ずっと all year 一年中, 一年を通して and all that ~とか何とか at all まったく(~ない) with all one's might 全身全霊をこめて

Word List

- **almost** 副 ほとんど, もう少しで(~するところ)
- **alone** 副 ひとりで, ~だけで
- **along** 前 ~に沿って 副 ~に沿って, 前へ, 進んで along with ~と一緒に
- **already** 副 すでに, もう
- **also** 副 ~も(また), ~も同様に
- **always** 副 いつも, 常に
- **am** 動 ~である, (~に)いる[ある]《主語がIのときのbeの現在形》
- **an** 冠 1つの, 1人の, ある
- **and** 接 ①そして, ~と… ②《同じ語を結んで》ますます ③《結果を表して》それで, だから and all that ~とか何とか
- **anger** 名 怒り
- **angrily** 副 怒って, 腹立たしげに
- **angry** 形 怒って, 腹を立てて be angry at ~に腹を立てている
- **animal** 名 動物
- **another** 形 ①もう1つ[1人]の ②別の yet another さらにもう一つの
- **answer** 動 答える, 応じる 名 答え, 返事
- **any** 形 ①《疑問文で》何か, いくつかの ②《否定文で》何も, 少しも(~ない) ③《肯定文で》どの~も 代 ①《疑問文で》(~のうち)何か, どれか, 誰か ②《否定文で》少しも, 何も[誰も]~ない ③《肯定文で》どれも, 誰でも not ~ any more もう[これ以上]~ない
- **anybody** 代 《疑問文・条件節で》誰か
- **anymore** 副 《通例否定文, 疑問文で》これ以上, これから
- **anyone** 代 《否定文で》誰にも
- **anything** 代 ①《疑問文で》何か, どれでも ②《否定文で》何も, どれも(~ない) ③《肯定文で》何でも, どれでも anything else ほかの何か
- **anywhere** 副 どこにも
- **are** 動 ~である, (~に)いる[ある]《主語がyou, we, theyまたは複数名詞のときのbeの現在形》
- **area** 名 区域, 場所
- **around** 副 ①まわりに, あちこちに ②およそ, 約 前 ~のまわりに, ~のあちこちに
- **arrest** 動 逮捕する
- **arrive** 動 到着する arrive at ~に着く
- **as** 接 ①《as ~ as …の形で》…と同じくらい~ ②~のとおりに, ~のように ③~しながら, ~しているときに ④~するにつれて, ~にしたがって ⑤~なので ⑥~だけれども ⑦~する限りでは 前 ①~として(の) ②~の時 同じくらい 代 ①~のような ②~だが as if あたかも~のように, まるで~みたいに as long as さえすれば as soon as ~するとすぐ, ~するや否や as though あたかも~のように, まるで~みたいに as usual いつものように as well なお, 同様に as ~ as one can できる限り~ as ~ as possible できるだけ~ so kind as to 親切にも~する
- **ask** 動 ①尋ねる, 聞く ②頼む, 求める ask ~ if ~かどうか尋ねる
- **asleep** 形 眠って(いる状態の) 副 眠って fall asleep 眠り込む, 寝入る fall fast asleep ぐっすりと寝入る
- **at** 前 ①《場所・時》~に[で] ②《目標・方向》~に[を], ~に向かって ③《原因・理由》~を見て[聞いて・知って] ④~に従事して, ~の状態で at all まったく(~ない) at this これを見て, そこで(すぐに)
- **ate** 動 eat(食べる)の過去
- **audience** 名 聴衆
- **away** 副 離れて, 遠くに, 去って 形 離れた far away 遠く離れて right away すぐに
- **awful** 形 ひどい, 恐ろしい

Short Stories of Kenji Miyazawa

B

- **baby** 名 ①赤ん坊 ②《呼びかけで》あなた 形 ①赤ん坊の ②小さな
- **back** 名 ①背中 ②裏, 後ろ 副 ①戻って ②後ろへ[に] 形 裏の, 後ろの back and forth 前後に call back 呼び返す go back to ～に帰る[戻る] hold back 阻害する put back (もとの場所に)戻す, 返す
- **bad** 形 悪い, へたな, まずい bad luck 災難, 不運
- **badger** 名 アナグマ
- **badly** 副 とても, ひどく
- **bag** 名 袋, かばん
- **bang** 名 バン[ドスン・バタン]という音
- **barber** 名 理髪師, 床屋
- **bark** 名 木の皮 動 ほえる, どなる
- **bath** 名 風呂
- **be** 動 ～である, (～に)いる[ある], ～となる 助 ①《現在分詞とともに用いて》～している ②《過去分詞とともに用いて》～される, ～されている
- **beat** 名 拍子, ビート
- **beautiful** 形 美しい, すばらしい
- **became** 動 become (なる)の過去
- **because** 接 (なぜなら)～だから, ～という理由[原因]で because of ～のために, ～のせいで
- **become** 動 (～に)なる
- **bed** 名 寝台, ベッド
- **been** 動 be (～である)の過去分詞 助 be (～している・～される)の過去分詞
- **before** 前 ～の前に[で], ～より以前に 接 ～する前に 副 以前に day before yesterday おととい
- **began** 動 begin (始まる)の過去
- **beginning** 動 begin (始まる)の現在分詞 名 初め, 始まり
- **behind** 前 ①～の後ろに, ～の背後に ②～に遅れて 副 ①後ろに, 背後に ②遅れて
- **believe** 動 信じる, 信じている
- **bell** 名 鈴, 鐘
- **belly** 名 腹 動 ふくらます, ふくらむ
- **beneath** 前 ～の下に
- **best** 形 最もよい, 最大[多]の 副 最もよく, 最も上手に 名 《the－》最上のもの
- **better** 形 ①よりよい ②(人が)回復して 副 よりよく, より上手に feel better 気分がよくなる, 元気になる
- **between** 前 (2つのもの)の間に[で・の]
- **beyond** 副 向こうに
- **big** 形 ①大きい ②偉い, 重要な 副 大きく, 大いに be no bigger than ～ほどの大きさだ
- **bird** 名 鳥
- **bit** 名 ①小片, 少量 ②《a－》少し, ちょっと ③部分
- **black** 形 黒い 名 黒, 黒色
- **blew** 動 blow (吹く)の過去
- **block** 動 さえぎる
- **blue** 形 青い 名 青(色)
- **body** 名 体, 胴体
- **bone** 名 骨
- **boot** 名 《-s》長靴, ブーツ
- **both** 形 両方の, 2つとものもの 副 《both ～ and … の形で》～も …も両方とも
- **bottle** 名 瓶
- **bought** 動 buy (買う)の過去, 過去分詞
- **bow** 動 (～に)お辞儀する 名 ①お辞儀, えしゃく ②弓, 弓状のもの
- **bowl** 名 おわん, ボウル
- **box** 名 箱, 容器
- **bread** 名 パン
- **break** 動 ①壊す ②(法律・約束を)破る
- **breakfast** 名 朝食
- **bright** 形 輝いている, 鮮明な

Word List

- **bring** 動持ってくる
- **British** 形英国人の
- **broke** 動break（壊す）の過去
- **broken** 動break（壊す）の過去分詞 形破れた，壊れた
- **brought** 動bring（持ってくる）の過去，過去分詞
- **brown** 形茶色の
- **brush** 名ブラシ 動ブラシをかける
- **Buddha** 名仏陀，釈迦《仏教の開祖》
- **building** 名建物
- **burned** 動燃えた
- **busily** 副忙しく，せっせと
- **business** 名仕事，用事
- **busy** 形忙しい
- **but** 接①でも，しかし ②～を除いて 前～を除いて，～のほかは 副ただ，のみ，ほんの **nothing but** ～のほかは何も…ない
- **button** 名ボタン
- **buy** 動買う
- **by** 前①《位置》～のそばに［で］②《手段・方法・行為者・基準》～によって，～で ③《期限》～までには ④《通過・経由》～を経由して，～を通って 副そばに，通り過ぎて **by the time** ～する時までに **by this time** もうすでに

C

- **call** 動呼ぶ，叫ぶ **call back** 呼び返す **call for** ～を呼び求める，呼び出す **call out** 叫ぶ，声を掛ける **call to** ～に声をかける
- **came** 動come（来る）の過去
- **can** 助①～できる ②～してもよい ③～でありうる ④《否定文で》～のはずがない **as ～ as one can** できる限り～ **can't help** ～せずにはいられない **Can you ～？** ～してくれますか。
- **cape** 名肩マント，ケープ **straw cape** みの《わら製の雨具》
- **care** 名世話 動①《通例否定文・疑問文で》気にする，心配する ②世話をする **take care of** ～の世話をする
- **careful** 形注意深い，慎重な
- **carry** 動運ぶ，連れていく，持ち歩く **carry ～ off** ～を運び去る **carry ～ out of** …から～を運び出す
- **case** 名①事件，問題 ②箱
- **cat** 名ネコ（猫）
- **catch** 動つかまえる
- **catfish** 名ナマズ（鯰）《魚》
- **caught** 動catch（つかまえる）の過去，過去分詞
- **ceiling** 名天井
- **cellist** 名チェロ奏者
- **cello** 名チェロ
- **chair** 名いす
- **change** 動変わる，変える
- **chapped** 形（肌が）荒れた
- **cheap** 形（値段が）安い，質の悪い
- **cheer** 動①元気づける ②かっさいを送る **cheer up** 元気になる，気分が引き立つ
- **chicken** 名ニワトリ（鶏），鶏肉
- **chief** 名頭，長 **police chief** 警察署長
- **child** 名子ども
- **children** 名child（子ども）の複数
- **chosen** 動choose（選ぶ）の過去分詞
- **cigarette** 名（紙巻）たばこ
- **circle** 名円，円周，輪 **run in circle** ぐるぐる走る
- **circulation** 名血行，血液循環
- **city** 名都市，都会
- **clang** 名カーン（という金属質の音）
- **clap** 動（手を）たたく 名手をたたくこと

Short Stories of Kenji Miyazawa

- **clarinet** 名 クラリネット
- **clean** 形 きれいな, 清潔な 動 よごれを落とす clean ~ off (汚れなどを)落とす
- **clear** 形 澄んだ
- **climb** 動 登る climb in through よじ登って~に入る climb out of ~から抜け出す
- **close** 副 接近して 動 閉まる, 閉じる
- **closely** 副 入念に, しっかりと
- **cloud** 名 雲
- **coat** 名 外套, コート
- **coin** 名 硬貨, コイン
- **cold** 形 寒い, 冷たい 名 風邪 have a cold 風邪を引いている
- **color** 名 色, 色彩
- **come** 動 ①来る, 行く, 現れる ②(出来事が)起こる, 生じる ③~になる ④comeの過去分詞 come across ~に出くわす, ~に遭遇する come and ~しに行く come back 戻ってくる come by やって来る come in 中に入る, やってくる, 加わる come into ~に入ってくる come on さあ来なさい come out 出てくる, 姿を現す come running 飛んでくる, かけつける come through 通り抜ける come up 浮上する, 発生する come up with ~を思いつく, 見つけ出す
- **comfortable** 形 快適な, 心地いい make oneself comfortable くつろぐ
- **conductor** 名 指導者, 指揮者
- **continue** 動 続く, 続ける continue on one's way 進み続ける
- **cook** 動 料理する
- **cool** 形 涼しい, 冷えた
- **corner** 名 すみ
- **cost** 名 値段, 費用 動 (金・費用が)かかる
- **could** 助 ①can (~できる)の過去 ②《控え目な推量・可能性・願望などを表す》Could you ~? ~してくださいますか。 If +《主語》+ could ~ できればなあ《仮定法》could have done ~だったかもしれない《仮定法》
- **country** 名《the-》田舎, 郊外
- **course** 名 of course もちろん, 当然
- **court** 名 法廷, 裁判所
- **crackle** 動 (火が)パチパチ音を立てる
- **crash** 動 ぶつかる, 砕ける crash into each other 互いに真っ向からぶつかる
- **cream** 名 乳脂, クリーム
- **cream-covered** 形 クリームまみれの
- **criminal** 名 犯罪者, 犯人
- **crumple** 動 しわくちゃ[ぺしゃんこ]になる
- **cry** 動 泣く, 叫ぶ, 嘆く cry out 叫ぶ
- **cuckoo** 名 カッコウ (の鳴き声)
- **cure** 動 治療する, 癒す
- **curtain** 名 (劇場の) 幕
- **customer** 名 顧客
- **cut** 動 ①切る, 刈る ②cutの過去, 過去分詞 cut down 切り倒す cut ~ off ~を切断する

D

- **dangerous** 形 危険な
- **dark** 形 暗い, 闇の
- **darkly** 副 陰気に
- **darkness** 名 暗さ, 暗やみ
- **day** 名 ①日中, 昼間 ②日, 期日 all day 一日中 all day long 一日中, 終日 day before yesterday おととい every day 毎日 one day ある日 the other day 先日
- **dead** 形 死んでいる

Word List

- **dear** 間 まあ, おや
- **death** 名 死 be sentenced to death 死刑判決を受ける to death 死ぬまで, 死ぬほど
- **decide** 動 決定[決意]する decide to do ～することに決める
- **deep** 形 深い 副 深く, 内奥に
- **deer** 名 シカ(鹿)
- **detective** 名 探偵
- **did** 動 do (～をする)の過去 助 do の過去
- **die** 動 死ぬ, 消滅する die of ～がもとで死ぬ
- **difference** 名 違い, 差
- **different** 形 異なった, 違った
- **difficult** 形 困難な, むずかしい
- **disappear** 動 見えなくなる, 姿を消す, なくなる disappear into thin air 虚空に消える
- **discover** 動 発見する
- **dish** 名 皿
- **dizzy** 形 めまいがする, 目が回る
- **do** 助 ①《ほかの動詞とともに用いて現在形の否定文・疑問文をつくる》②《同じ動詞を繰り返す代わりに用いる》③《動詞を強調するのに用いる》動 ～をする ド《音階》 do a good job うまくやってのける don't have to ～する必要はない Why don't you ～? ～したらどうだい, ～しませんか。
- **does** 動 do (～をする)の3人称単数現在 助 doの3人称単数現在
- **dog** 名 犬
- **dollar** 名 ドル《米国などの通貨単位》
- **done** 動 do (～をする)の過去分詞 well done うまくやった
- **door** 名 扉, 戸, ドア
- **down** 副 ①下へ, 降りて, 低くなって ②倒れて 前 ～の下方へ, ～を下って 形 下方の, 下りの put down 下に置く, 下ろす roll down 転がり落ちる run down (液体が)流れ落ちる, 駆け下りる, (車で人を)ひく set down ～を下に置く, ～と見なす take down 下げる, 降ろす up and down 上がったり下がったり, 行ったり来たり, あちこちと write down 書き留める
- **Dream on.** 勝手に言ってろよ。《皮肉》
- **dress** 動 服を着る[着せる]
- **drink** 動 飲む
- **drive** 動 追いやる drive ～ away ～を追い払う
- **driver** 名 (馬車の) 御者
- **drop** 動 落ちる, 落下する hear a pin drop (ピンの落ちる音が聞こえるくらい) 静かだ
- **drum** 名 太鼓, ドラム
- **drunk** 動 drink (飲む)の過去分詞
- **dry** 動 乾燥する[させる], 干す
- **during** 前 ～の間 (ずっと)

E

- **each** 形 それぞれの, 各自の each other お互いに
- **ear** 名 耳, 聴覚
- **early** 副 早くに
- **earth** 名 地球, この世 what on earth 一体全体
- **east** 名 《the –》東
- **eat** 動 食べる, 食事する
- **eaten** 動 eat (食べる)の過去分詞
- **eel** 名 ウナギ(鰻)
- **eight** 名 8 (の数字)
- **either** 形 どちらでも 副 《否定文で》～もまた (…ない)
- **electricity** 名 電気
- **elephant** 名 象
- **else** 副 そのほかに[の] anything else ほかの何か
- **encore** 名 アンコール

Short Stories of Kenji Miyazawa

- □ **end** 名終わり, 果て 動終わる, 終える **end up** 最後には〜することになる **in the end** とうとう, 結局, ついに
- □ **energy** 名勢い, 精力, エネルギー
- □ **enjoy** 動楽しむ **enjoy doing** 〜するのを楽しむ
- □ **enough** 形十分な, (〜するのに)足る 副(〜できる)だけ, 十分に, まったく **enough to do** 〜するのに十分な **have ehough** 堪能する, 満喫する **That's enough out of you.** いいかげんにしなさい。 **well enough** かなり上手に
- □ **enter** 動入る
- □ **especially** 副とりわけ
- □ **esquire** 名〜殿《古》
- □ **estimate** 動見積もる
- □ **even** 副《強意》〜でさえも, 〜ですら, さらに
- □ **evening** 名夕方, 晩
- □ **ever** 副①今までに ②《強意》絶対に **ever again** 二度と
- □ **every** 形①どの〜も, すべての, あらゆる ②毎〜, 〜ごとの **every day** 毎日 **every time** 〜するときはいつも
- □ **everybody** 代誰でも, 皆
- □ **everyone** 代誰でも, 皆
- □ **everything** 代すべてのこと[もの], 何でも, 何もかも
- □ **everywhere** 副どこも
- □ **excited** 動excite (興奮する)の過去, 過去分詞 形興奮した, わくわくした **get excited** 興奮する
- □ **excuse** 動許す, 容赦する **excuse me** すみません
- □ **experienced** 形熟練の
- □ **explain** 動説明する
- □ **eye** 名目

F

- □ **fa** 名ファ《音階》
- □ **face** 名顔
- □ **fact** 名事実, 真相 **in fact** つまり, 実は, 要するに
- □ **fall** 動①落ちる, 倒れる ②(ある状態に)急に陥る 名滝 **fall asleep** 眠り込む, 寝入る **fall behind** 遅れをとる **fall down** 転ぶ **fall fast asleep** ぐっすりと寝入る **fall to the ground** 転ぶ
- □ **far** 副大いに, 遠くに 形遠い, 向こうの **far away** 遠く離れて
- □ **farther** 副もっと遠く, さらに先に **farther on** もっと先に
- □ **fast** 副①速く ②しっかりと **fall fast asleep** ぐっすりと寝入る
- □ **fat** 形太った
- □ **father** 名父親
- □ **fear** 名恐れ **in fear** おどおどして, ビクビクして
- □ **feel** 動感じる, (〜と)思う **feel better** 気分がよくなる, 元気になる **feel free** 遠慮なしに, 気兼ねせず **feel like** 〜したい気がする, 〜のような感じがする **feel sorry for** 〜をかわいそうに思う **not feel like doing** 〜する気になれない
- □ **feeling** 動feel (感じる)の現在分詞 名①感じ, 気持ち ②触感
- □ **feet** 名foot (足)の複数 **on one's feet** 立っている状態で
- □ **fell** 動fall (落ちる)の過去
- □ **felt** 動feel (感じる)の過去, 過去分詞
- □ **few** 形《a-》少しの, わずかの
- □ **field** 名野原, 田畑
- □ **fifth-grader** 名五年生
- □ **fifteen** 名15(の数字)
- □ **fight** 動(〜と)争う
- □ **figure out** (原因などを)解明する
- □ **fill** 動①満ちる, 満たす ②《be -ed with 〜》〜でいっぱいである **fill up**

Word List

(穴・すき間を)いっぱいに満たす, 詰める
- **find** 動①見つける ②(〜と)わかる, 気づく, 〜と考える find oneself いつの間にか〜している
- **fine** 形①美しい, りっぱな, 申し分ない, 結構な ②細かい 副りっぱに, 申し分なく
- **finger** 名(手の)指
- **finish** 動終わる, 終える finish doing 〜するのを終える
- **fire** 名火
- **first** 名最初 形第一の, 最初の 副第一に, 最初に at first 最初は, 初めのうちは
- **fish** 名魚 動釣りをする
- **fishing** 動fish(釣りをする)の現在分詞 名釣り, 漁業
- **fit** 動(大きさが)合う
- **fix** 動〜に仕返しをする
- **flat** 形平坦な, のっぺりした, 単調な
- **flew** 動fly(飛ぶ)の過去
- **floor** 名床
- **flown** 動fly(飛ぶ)の過去分詞
- **flute** 名フルート《楽器》
- **fly** 動①飛ぶ, 飛ばす ②(飛ぶように)過ぎる, 急ぐ fly open パッと開く fly out of 〜から飛び出す
- **follow** 動①ついていく ②(規則などに)従う ③(仕事などに)従事する
- **food** 名食物
- **foot** 名足 on one's feet 立っている状態で stamp one's foot 足を踏み鳴らす
- **for** 前①《目的・原因・対象》〜にとって, 〜のために[の], 〜に対して ②《期間》〜間 ③《代理》〜の代わりに ④《方向》〜へ(向かって) 接というわけは〜, なぜなら〜, だから for now 今のところ, ひとまず
- **forest** 名森林

- **forever** 副永遠に
- **forgot** 動forget(忘れる)の過去, 過去分詞
- **fork** 名フォーク
- **form** 動形づくる
- **forth** 副前へ back and forth 前後に
- **forward** 副前方に step forward 進み出る
- **found** 動find(見つける)の過去, 過去分詞
- **four** 名4(の数字)
- **free** 形自由な 副自由に feel free 遠慮なしに, 気兼ねせず
- **fresh** 形さわやかな
- **friend** 名友だち, 仲間
- **from** 前①《出身・出発点・時間・順序・原料》〜から ②《原因・理由》〜がもとで from now on 今後 from side to side 左右に from then on それ以来 from time to time ときどき from 〜 to 〜から…まで
- **front** 名正面, 前 形正面の, 前面の in front of 〜の前に, 〜の正面に
- **full** 形満ちた, いっぱいの be full of 〜で一杯である
- **fun** 名楽しみ, おもしろいこと 形楽しい, ゆかいな make fun of 〜を物笑いの種にする, からかう
- **funny** 形①おもしろい ②奇妙な
- **future** 名未来 in the future 将来は

G

- **gather** 動集まる
- **gave** 動give(与える)の過去
- **gentleman** 名紳士
- **gentlemen** 名gentleman(紳士)の複数
- **get** 動①得る, 手に入れる ②(ある状態に)なる, いたる ③わかる, 理解

Short Stories of Kenji Miyazawa

する ④〜させる,〜を(…の状態に)する ⑤(ある場所に)達する,着く **get down** 身をかがめる,ひざまずく **get excited** 興奮する **get far** 遠くまで行く **get home** 家に着く[帰る] **get into** 〜に入る **get it right** きんとやる **get mad at** 〜に腹を立てる **get on** (電車などに)乗る,気が合う **get out of** 〜から外へ出る **get ready** 用意[支度]をする **get sick** 病気になる,気分が悪くなる **get through** 通過する **get to do** 〜できるようになる,〜できる機会を得る

☐ **give** 動 ①与える,贈る ②(〜を)する **give an order** 命令する **give it a try** 試しにやってみる

☐ **glad** 形 うれしい,喜ばしい

☐ **glass** 名 ①ガラス(状のもの),コップ,グラス ②《-es》めがね

☐ **go** 動 ①行く,出かける ②動く ③進む,経過する,いたる ④(ある状態に)なる **be going to** 〜するつもりである **go ahead** さあ〜しなさい **go around** 動き回る **go away** 立ち去る **go back to** 〜に帰る[戻る] **go doing** 〜をしに行く **go home** 帰宅する **go in** 中に入る,開始する **go into** 〜に入る **go on** 続く,続ける,起こる **go out** 外出する,外へ出る **go past** 通り過ぎる **go through** 通り抜ける **have got to** 〜しなければならない

☐ **gold** 形 金の,金色の

☐ **gone** 動 go(行く)の過去分詞

☐ **good** 形 ①よい,上手な,優れた,美しい ②(数量・程度が)かなりの,相当な **be not good for** 〜に良くない **do a good job** うまくやってのける

☐ **good-for-nothing** 形 役立たずな

☐ **goodness** 間 やれやれ

☐ **Gorsch** 名 ゴーシュ《人名》

☐ **got** 動 get(得る)の過去,過去分詞 **have got to** 〜しなければならない

☐ **gotten** 動 get(得る)の過去分詞

☐ **grader** 名 〜年生,〜学年の生徒

☐ **grandmother** 名 祖母

☐ **grass** 名 草,芝生

☐ **gray** 形 灰色の

☐ **great** 形 ①大きい,広大な,(量や程度が)たいへんな ②偉大な,優れた ③すばらしい,おもしろい

☐ **green** 形 緑色の

☐ **grew** 動 grow(成長する)の過去

☐ **ground** 名 地面,土 **fall to the ground** 転ぶ **on the ground** 地面に

☐ **group** 名 集団,群

☐ **growl** 動 (〜に向かって)うなる

☐ **guess** 動 推測する,(〜と)思う

☐ **guest** 名 客

☐ **guide** 名 案内人,ガイド

☐ **gun** 名 銃,鉄砲

H

☐ **had** 動 have(持つ)の過去,過去分詞 助 have の過去《過去完了の文をつくる》

☐ **hair** 名 髪

☐ **hall** 名 公会堂,玄関ホール

☐ **hand** 名 手 動 手渡す

☐ **handwriting** 名 筆跡,書体

☐ **hang** 動 かかる,ぶら下がる **hanging on** 〜にかかっている **hang one's head** うなだれる

☐ **happen** 動 ①(出来事が)起こる,生じる ②偶然[たまたま]〜する **happen to** たまたま〜する,偶然〜する

☐ **happily** 副 幸福に,喜んで

☐ **happy** 形 幸せな,うれしい

☐ **hard** 形 むずかしい 副 ①一生懸命に ②激しく **hard to** 〜し難い

☐ **has** 動 have(持つ)の3人称単数現在 助 have の3人称単数現在《現在完

Word List

了の文をつくる》
- **hat** 名(縁のある)帽子
- **have** 動①持つ, 持っている, 抱く ②(〜が)ある, いる ③食べる, 飲む ④経験する, (病気に)かかる ⑤催す, 開く ⑥(人に)〜させる 動《〈have + 過去分詞〉の形で現在完了の文をつくる》〜した, 〜したことがある, ずっと〜している could have done 〜だったかもしれない《仮定法》 don't have to 〜する必要はない have a cold 風邪を引いている have got to 〜しなければならない have no idea わからない should have done 〜すべきだった(のにしなかった)《仮定法》
- **he** 代彼は[が]
- **head** 名①頭 ②(集団の)長 動向かう hang one's head うなだれる head back 引き返す
- **health** 名健康(状態)
- **hear** 動聞く, 聞こえる hear about 〜について聞く hear a pin drop (ピンの落ちる音が聞こえるくらい)静かだ hear of 〜について聞く
- **heard** 動 hear (聞く)の過去, 過去分詞
- **heavy** 形重い, 激しい heavy with sleep (まぶたなどが)眠くて重い
- **held** 動 hold (つかむ)の過去, 過去分詞
- **hell** 名地獄
- **hello** 間こんにちは, やあ
- **help** 動①助ける, 手伝う ②給仕する can't help 〜せずにはいられない help oneself 自由に取って食べる[飲む]
- **helper** 名お手伝い
- **her** 代①彼女を[に] ②彼女の
- **here** 副①ここに[で] ②《〈- is [are] 〜〉》ここに〜がある ③さあ, そら 名ここ
- **heroic** 形壮大な
- **hey** 間《呼びかけ・注意を促して》おい, ちょっと
- **hide** 動隠れる
- **high** 形高い
- **hill** 名丘
- **him** 代彼を[に]
- **himself** 代彼自身
- **his** 代①彼の ②彼のもの
- **hiss** 動(シューと)音を出す
- **hit** 動①打つ, なぐる ②ぶつける, ぶつかる ③命中する ④hitの過去, 過去分詞
- **hmm** 間ふむ, ううむ《熟考・疑問・ためらいなどを表す》
- **hold** 動①つかむ, 持つ, 抱く ②保持する hold back 阻害する hold onto 〜にしがみつく
- **hole** 名穴, すき間
- **home** 名家 副家に get home 家に着く[帰る] go home 帰宅する take someone home (人)を家まで送る
- **honor** 名名誉
- **hope** 動望む, (〜であるようにと)思う
- **horse** 名馬 Day of the Horse 午の日
- **hospital** 名病院
- **hot** 形暑い, 熱い
- **house** 名家
- **how** 副①どうやって, どれくらい, どんなふうに ②なんて(〜だろう) ③《関係副詞》〜する方法 How about 〜? 〜はどうですか。 how to 〜する方法 no matter how どんなに〜であろうとも
- **however** 接けれども, だが
- **hundred** 名100(の数字)
- **hung** 動 hang (かかる)の過去, 過去分詞
- **hunger** 名空腹, 飢え
- **hungry** 形空腹の, 飢えた
- **hunt** 動狩りをする 名狩り

Short Stories of Kenji Miyazawa

- **hunter** 名 狩人, 猟師
- **hurry** 動 急ぐ, 急がせる, あわてる 名 急ぐこと, 急ぐ必要 **hurry up** 急ぐ **in a hurry** 急いで, あわてて
- **hurt** 動 傷つける, 痛む

I

- **I** 代 私は [が]
- **ice** 名 氷
- **Ichiro Kaneta** かねた一郎《人名》
- **idea** 名 考え, 意見, アイデア **have no idea** わからない
- **if** 接 もし~ならば, たとえ~でも, ~かどうか **If +《主語》+ could** ~できればなあ《仮定法》 **as if** あたかも~のように, まるで~みたいに **ask if** ~かどうか尋ねる **see if** ~かどうかを確かめる **wonder if** ~ではないかと思う
- **important** 形 重要な, 大切な, 有力な
- **impossible** 形 できない, あり [起こり] えない
- **in** 前 ①《場所・位置・所属》~ (の中) で [で・の] ②《時》~ (の時) に [の・で], ~後 (に), ~の間 (に) ③《方法・手段》~で ④~を身につけて, ~を着て ⑤~に関して, ~について ⑥《状態》~の状態で 副 中へ [に], 内へ [に]
- **inch** 名 インチ《長さの単位。1/12フィート, 2.54cm》
- **increase** 動 増える
- **India** 名 インド《国名》
- **ink** 名 墨, インク
- **inn** 名 宿屋
- **inside** 名 内部, 内側 副 内部 [内側] に 前 ~の内部 [内側] に
- **instead of** ~の代わりに, ~をしないで
- **instrument** 名 楽器
- **interesting** 形 おもしろい, 興味を起こさせる
- **into** 前 ①《動作・運動の方向》~の中へ [に] ②《変化》~に [へ]
- **is** 動 be (~である) の3人称単数現在
- **it** 代 ①それは [が], それを [に] ②《天候・日時・距離・寒暖などを示す》**It is ~ of A to A** …するのは~だ **It takes ~ to** …するのに~ (時間など) がかかる **That's it.** それだけのことだ。
- **its** 代 それの, あれの

J

- **jazz** 名 ジャズ
- **job** 名 仕事 **do a good job** うまくやってのける
- **join** 動 ①一緒になる, 参加する ②連結 [結合] する, つなぐ **join in** 加わる
- **joy** 名 喜び
- **judge** 動 判決を下す, 裁く 名 判事
- **jump** 動 跳ぶ, 跳躍する, 飛びかかる **jump into the air** 空中に飛び上がる **jump up** 素早く立ち上がる **jump up and down** 飛び跳ねる
- **just** 形 正しい, もっともな, 当然な 副 ①まさに, ちょうど, (~した) ばかり ②ほんの, 単に, ただ~だけ ③ちょっと **just as** ~と全く同じように, ~の通りに, ~と同じくらいに **just then** そのとたんに

K

- **Karakon Mountain** カラコン山
- **keep** 動 ①続ける ②(~を…に) しておく **keep still** じっとしている
- **kept** keep (とっておく) の過去, 過去分詞
- **keyhole** 名 かぎ穴
- **kick** 動 ける, キックする

Word List

- **kill** 動殺す
- **kind** 形親切な, 優しい 名種類 kind of ~のようなもの so kind as to 親切にも~する
- **kindly** 副どうか~
- **kitchen** 名台所, 調理場
- **knew** 動know (知っている) の過去
- **knife** 名ナイフ, 小刀
- **knock** 動たたく, ノックする 名戸をたたくこと [音], ノック
- **know** 動①知っている, 知る, (~が) わかる, 理解している ②知り合いである be known as ~として知られている you know ご存知のとおり, あのね, ほら
- **known** 動know (知っている) の過去分詞 形知られた

L

- **la** 名ラ《音階》
- **laid** 動lay (置く) の過去, 過去分詞
- **lake** 名湖, 池
- **land** 名陸地, 土地 動上陸する, 着地する
- **large** 形大きい, 広い
- **last** 形①《the –》最後の ②この前の, 先~ 名《the –》最後, 終わり at last ついに, 最後に, ようやく
- **late** 形遅い 副①遅れて, 遅く ②夜遅くまで
- **later** 副後で, 後ほど
- **laugh** 動笑う 名笑い (声) laugh at ~を見て [聞いて] 笑う
- **law** 名法, 法律
- **lay** 動lie (横たわる) の過去
- **lead** 動導く, (道などが) 通じる lead the way 先に立って導く
- **leader** 名指導者, リーダー
- **learn** 動学ぶ, 教わる

- **least** 形いちばん小さい, 最も少ない 名最小, 最少 at least 少なくとも, せめて
- **leave** 動①去る, 出発する ②~を残す, 置いていく ③(~を…の) ままにしておく leave ~ out ~を除外する
- **led** 動lead (導く) の過去, 過去分詞
- **left** 動leave (去る, ~をあとに残す) の過去, 過去分詞
- **let** 動(人に~) させる, (~するのを) 許す, (~をある状態に) する Let me see. ええと.
- **letter** 名①手紙 ②文字
- **lie** 動①うそをつく ②横たわる, 寝る lie down 横たわる, 横になる
- **light** 名光, 明かり 動火をつける 形明るい
- **lighter** 形light (明るい) の比較級
- **like** 動好む, 好きである 前~に似ている, ~のような 形似ている, ~のような 接あたかも~のように 名①好きなもの ②《the [one's] –》同じようなもの [人] Would you like ~? はいかがですか. feel like ~したい気がする, ~のような感じがする like this このような, こんなふうに look like ~のように見える not feel like doing ~する気になれない sound like ~のように聞こえる would like to ~したいと思う
- **line** 名小節
- **lion** 名ライオン
- **listen** 動《– to ~》~を聞く, ~に耳を傾ける
- **lit** 動light (火をつける) の過去, 過去分詞
- **little** 形①小さい, 幼い ②少しの, 短い ③ほとんど~ない, 《a –》少しはある 名少し (しか), 少量 副全然~ない, 《a –》少しはある
- **live** 動住む, 暮らす
- **lock** 名錠 (前) 動錠を下ろす
- **long** 形①長い, 長期の ②《長さ・

Short Stories of Kenji Miyazawa

- **look** 動①見る ②(~に)見える, (~の)顔つきをする ③注意する ④《間投詞のように》ほら, ねえ look away 横を向く look down 見下ろす, うつむく look into ~をのぞき込む look like ~のように見える look up 見上げる
- **lost** 動 lose (失う)の過去, 過去分詞
- **lot** 名 たくさん, たいへん, 《a – of ~ / -s of ~》たくさんの~
- **loud** 形 大声の, 騒がしい 副 大声に[で]
- **loudly** 副 騒がしく
- **love** 動 大好きである would love to do ~したい
- **lovely** 形 美しい, すばらしい
- **low** 形 低い
- **luck** 名 運, めぐり合わせ bad luck 災難, 不運
- **lucky** 形 幸運な, 運のよい
- **lying** 動 lie (横たわる)の現在分詞

M

- **mad** 形 頭にきて get mad at ~に腹を立てる
- **made** 動 make (作る)の過去, 過去分詞 形 作った, 作られた be made of ~でできて[作られて]いる
- **main** 形 主な, 主要な
- **make** 動①作る, 得る ②行う, (~に)なる ③(~を…に)する, (~を…)させる make fun of ~を物笑いの種にする, からかう make noise 音を立てる make oneself comfortable くつろぐ make sure 確実に~する make up one's mind 決心する make up with ~と仲直りする make ~ into ~を…に仕立てる

距離・時間などを示す語句を伴って》~の長さ[距離・時間] 副 長い間, ずっと all day long 一日中, 終日 as long as ~さえすれば

- **man** 名 男性, 人
- **manager** 名 経営者, 支配人
- **many** 形 多数の, たくさんの so many 非常に多くの
- **maple** 名 カエデ(楓)《植物》
- **massage** 名 あんま, マッサージ
- **master** 名 主人, 師
- **match** 名 マッチ(棒)
- **matter** 名 問題 動 《主に疑問文・否定文で》重要である a matter of ~の問題 no matter how どんなに~であろうとも
- **may** 助 ~かもしれない
- **maybe** 副 たぶん, おそらく
- **mayor** 名 町長
- **me** 代 私を[に]
- **meal** 名 食事
- **mean** 動①意味する ②(~のもりで)言う, 意図する ③~するつもりである 形 けちな, 意地悪な
- **meeting** 動 meet (会う)の現在分詞
- **men** 名 man (男性)の複数
- **meow** 動 ニャーと鳴く
- **met** 動 meet (会う)の過去, 過去分詞
- **metal** 名 金属
- **mi** 名 ミ《音階》
- **mice** 名 mouse (ネズミ)の複数
- **middle** 名 中間, 最中 in the middle of ~の真ん中[中ほど]に
- **midnight** 名 夜の12時, 真夜中
- **might** 助《mayの過去》~かもしれない 名 力 with all one's might 全身全霊をこめて
- **mind** 名 心, 考え 動 気にする, いやがる make up one's mind 決心する
- **mine** 代 私のもの
- **minute** 名①(時間の)分 ②ちょっとの間 Wait a minute. ちょっと待って。

Word List

- **mirror** 名鏡
- **miss** 動(必要なものが)ない missing from ～からなくなっている
- **mistake** 名間違い
- **mix** 動混ぜる
- **moment** 名瞬間, ちょっとの間 for a moment 少しの間
- **money** 名金, 通貨
- **month** 名月, 1ヵ月
- **moon** 名月
- **more** 形①もっと多くの ②それ以上の, 余分の 副もっと, さらに多く, いっそう more than ～以上 not ～ any more もう［これ以上］～ない the more ～ the more ～すればするほどますます…
- **morning** 名朝, 午前 one morning ある朝
- **most** 形たいていの, 大部分の 代大部分, ほとんど 副最も(多く)
- **mother** 名母, 母親
- **mountain** 名山
- **mouse** 名(ハツカ)ネズミ
- **mouth** 名口
- **move** 動①動く, 動かす ②感動させる be moved 感激する, 感銘する
- **Mr.** 名《男性に対して》～さん, ～氏, ～先生
- **much** 形(量・程度が)多くの, 多量の 副①とても, たいへん ②《比較級・最上級を修飾して》ずっと, はるかに too much 過度の, やりすぎの
- **mud** 名泥
- **mushroom** 名キノコ
- **music** 名音楽, 楽譜
- **musician** 名音楽家
- **must** 助①～しなければならない ②～に違いない
- **my** 代私の
- **myself** 代私自身

N

- **named** 形～という名前の
- **near** 副近くに
- **need** 名必要(性) 助～する必要がある need to do ～する必要がある
- **neither** 副～もまた…ない
- **nervous** 形緊張した, 神経が高ぶった
- **never** 副決して［少しも］～ない, 一度も［二度と］～ない
- **new** 形新しい, 新人の
- **next** 形①次の, 翌～ ②隣の 副①次に ②隣に next time 次回に next to ～のとなりに
- **nice** 形すてきな, よい, 親切な
- **night** 名夜, 晩
- **no** 副①いいえ, いや ②少しも～ない 形～がない, 少しも～ない, ～禁止 be no bigger than ～ほどの大きさだ no matter how どんなに～であろうとも no one 誰も［一人も］～ない
- **nobody** 代誰も［1人も］～ない
- **noise** 名騒音, 騒ぎ, 物音 make noise 音を立てる
- **none** 代どれ一つとして～ない
- **nose** 名鼻
- **not** 副～でない, ～しない
- **note** 名音色, 音符
- **nothing** 代何も～ない［しない］ nothing but ～のほかは何も…ない
- **notice** 動気づく
- **now** 副①今(では), 現在 ②今すぐに ③では, さて 名今, 現在 for now 今のところ, ひとまず from now on 今後 right now 今すぐに, たった今
- **number** 名数, 数字
- **nut** 名木の実, ナッツ

O

- **oak** 名 オーク《ブナ科の樹木の総称》
- **ocean** 名 海
- **o'clock** 副 ～時
- **of** 前 ①《所有・所属・部分》～の, ～に属する ②《性質・特徴・材料》～の, ～製の ③《部分》～のうち ④《分離・除去》～から **of course** もちろん, 当然 **one of** ～の1つ[人] **out of** ①～から外へ, ～から抜け出して ②～から作り出して, ～を材料として ③～の範囲外に, ～から離れて ④(ある数)の中から
- **off** 副 ①離れて, 外れて ②(機能が)停止して 形 調子が悪い 前 ～を離れて
- **offer** 動 申し込む, 提供する
- **often** 副 しばしば, たびたび
- **oh** 間 ああ, おや, まあ
- **old** 形 ①年取った ②古い, 昔の
- **on** 前 ①《場所・接触》～(の上)に ②《日・時》～に, ～と同時に, ～のすぐ後で ③《関係・従事》～に関して, ～について, ～して 副 ①身につけて, 上に ②前へ, 続けて **on and on** 延々と
- **once** 副 ①一度, 1回 ②かつて **all at once** 突然, 出し抜けに
- **one** 名 1(の数字), 1人[個] 形 ①1の, 1人[個]の ②ある～ ③《the -》唯一の, 片方の 代 ①(一般の)人, ある物 ②～なもの **no one** 誰も[一人も]～ない **one after the other** 次々に, 順々に **one day** (過去の)ある日, (未来の)いつか **one morning** ある朝 **one of** ～の1つ[人] **this one** これ, こちら
- **only** 形 唯一の 副 ①単に, ～にすぎない, ただ～だけ ②やっと
- **onto** 前 ～の上へ[に]
- **open** 形 開いた 動 ①開く ②広がる, 広げる **fly open** パッと開く
- **or** 接 ～か…, または
- **orchestra** 名 管弦楽団, オーケストラ
- **order** 名 命令, 注文(品) **give an order** 命令する
- **other** 形 ①ほかの, 異なった ②(2つのうち)もう一方の, (3つ以上のうち)残りの 代 ①ほかの人[物] ②《the -》残りの1つ **each other** お互いに **one after the other** 次々に, 順々に **the other day** 先日
- **our** 代 私たちの
- **out** 副 ①外へ[に], 不在で, 離れて ②世に出て ③消えて ④すっかり 形 ①外の, ～を離れた ②公表された 前 ～から外へ[に] **out of** ①～から外へ, ～から抜け出して ②～から作り出して, ～を材料として ③～の範囲外に, ～から離れて ④(ある数)の中から
- **outside** 名 外部, 外側 副 外へ, 外側に
- **over** 前 ①～の上の[に], ～を一面に覆って ②～を越えて, ～以上に, ～よりまさって ③～の向こう側の[に] 副 上に, 一面に, ずっと **all over** ～中で, 全体にわたって, ～の至る所で **over and over** 何度も繰り返して **over and over again** 何度も繰り返して
- **owl** 名 フクロウ(梟), ミミズク
- **owner** 名 持ち主, オーナー

P

- **pack** 動 荷造りする, 詰め込む **pack up** 荷物をまとめる
- **page** 名 ページ
- **paid** 動 pay (払う)の過去, 過去分詞 形 有給の
- **paint** 動 ①ペンキを塗る ②(絵の具などで)描く
- **pants** 名 ズボン, スラックス
- **paper** 名 紙 **waste paper** 古紙
- **part** 名 部分
- **pass** 動 (年月が)たつ, 過ぎる
- **past** 前 《時間・場所》～を過ぎて,

Word List

~を越して 副 通り越して, 過ぎて
go past 通り過ぎる
- **path** 名 (踏まれてできた)小道, 歩道
- **pay** 動 支払う, 払う
- **payment** 名 報酬, 支払い
- **peaceful** 形 穏やかな
- **peacefully** 副 穏やかに
- **people** 名 (一般に)人々, 人間
- **perfect** 形 完璧な, 完全な
- **perfectly** 副 完全に, 申し分なく
- **performance** 名 演奏
- **perfume** 名 香水
- **person** 名 人
- **phew** 間 ふう!
- **pick** 動 (~を)摘み取る pick oneself up 元気を出す[回復する] pick up 拾い上げる
- **picture** 名 絵
- **piece** 名 ①一片, 部分 ②1つ ③作品
- **pin** 名 細い留め具, ピン hear a pin drop (ピンの落ちる音が聞こえるくらい)静かだ
- **pint** 名 パイント《単位:米国で約0.47リットル》
- **place** 名 場所, 建物
- **plain** 形 平凡な
- **play** 動 (楽器を)演奏する
- **player** 名 演奏者
- **please** 動 喜ばす, 満足させる 副 お願いだから, ぜひとも, なにとぞ 間 どうぞ, お願いします
- **point** 動 (~を)指す
- **pointed** 動 point (指す)の過去, 過去分詞 形 先のとがった, 鋭い
- **poison** 名 毒, 毒薬
- **poison-bag fishing** 毒もみ《川の中で毒の入った袋をもみ, 浮いた魚をとる漁法》
- **police** 名 ①《the -》警察, 官官 police chief 警察署長
- **policeman** 名 警察官
- **policemen** 名 policeman(警察官)の複数
- **pond** 名 池
- **poor** 形 ①貧しい, 粗末な ②不幸な, 気の毒な poor thing 気の毒な人
- **popular** 形 人気のある
- **possible** 形 可能な as ~ as possible できるだけ~
- **possibly** 副 《否定文で》とうてい~ない
- **pot** 名 壺
- **pour** 動 注ぐ, 浴びせる
- **powder** 名 粉末 動 粉砕する
- **powdered** 形 粉末の
- **practice** 名 練習 動 練習する
- **preacher** 名 説教師
- **presence** 名 出席
- **present** 名 贈り物, プレゼント
- **pretty** 副 非常に
- **primary school** 小学校
- **probably** 副 たぶん, おそらく
- **problem** 名 問題
- **profit** 名 利益
- **promise** 動 約束する
- **Puhara** 名 プハラ《地名》
- **pull** 動 引く, 引っ張る
- **purse** 名 財布, 小銭入れ
- **push** 動 ~を押す
- **put** 動 ①置く, のせる ②入れる, つける ③(ある状態に)する ④putの過去, 過去分詞 put back (もとの場所に)戻す, 返す put down 下に置く, 下ろす put ~ in ~を…の中に入れる put ~ into ~を…の状態にする, ~を…に突っ込む put ~ on ①~を身につける, 着る, (体に)塗る ②~を…の上に置く put on trial 裁判にかける put out 外に出す, (手など)を(差し)出す

Short Stories of Kenji Miyazawa

Q

- **quick** 形 (動作が)速い, すばやい
- **quickly** 副 敏速に, 急いで
- **quiet** 形 静かな, おとなしい 動 静まる quiet down 静かになる
- **quietly** 副 ①静かに ②控えめに
- **quite** 副 ①すっかり, 完全に ②かなり, ずいぶん

R

- **rabbit** 名 ウサギ(兎)
- **rain** 名 雨
- **ran** 動 run(走る)の過去
- **rang** 動 ring(鳴る)の過去
- **rather** 副 ①どちらかといえば ②いくぶん, やや
- **re** 名 レ《音階》
- **read** 動 読む, (文字が)書いてある
- **ready** 形 用意[準備]ができた get ready 用意[支度]をする
- **really** 副 本当に, 実際に, 確かに
- **reason** 名 理由 for some reason どういうわけか
- **receive** 動 受け取る
- **red** 形 赤い 名 赤, 赤色 turn red 赤くなる
- **remember** 動 思い出す
- **remind** 動 思い出させる
- **reply** 動 答える, 返事をする
- **rest** 名 休息 動 休む, 眠る
- **restaurant** 名 料理店, レストラン
- **return** 動 帰る, 戻る 名 返答 in return 返礼として
- **rich** 形 金持ちの
- **Richiki** 名 リチキ《人名》
- **right** 形 ①正しい ②適切な 副 ①まっすぐに, すぐに ②ちょうど, 正確に all right 大丈夫で, よろしい, わかった, 承知した right away すぐに right now 今すぐに, たった今
- **ring** 動 鳴らす
- **rise** 動 昇る, 上がる
- **river** 名 川
- **road** 名 道路, 道
- **robe** 名 (裁判官などの)法服, ローブ
- **rock** 名 岸壁, 岩石 動 揺らす
- **roll** 動 転がる roll around 転げ回る roll down 転がり落ちる
- **room** 名 部屋
- **rose** 動 rise(昇る)の過去
- **rough** 形 荒れた, ザラザラした
- **round** 形 丸い
- **royal** 形 皇族の
- **rule** 名 規則, ルール
- **run** 動 ①走る ②(川が)流れる come running 飛んでくる, かけつける run across 走って渡る run along 並んでいる run around 走り回る run away 走り去る, 逃げ出す run down (液体が)流れ落ちる run in 走って入る run in circle ぐるぐる走る run into ~に駆け込む, ~の中に走って入る run through 走り抜ける
- **Russian** 形 ロシア(人)の

S

- **sad** 形 悲しい, 悲しげな
- **sadly** 副 悲しそうに, 不幸にも
- **sadness** 名 悲しみ, 悲哀
- **safe** 形 安全な, 危険のない 名 金庫
- **safely** 副 間違いなく
- **said** 動 say(言う)の過去, 過去分詞
- **salt** 名 塩, 食塩 動 塩を振りかける, 塩漬けにする
- **same** 形 同じ, 同様の 副《the-》同様に
- **sang** 動 sing(歌う)の過去

Word List

- **sansho** 名 山椒《植物》
- **sat** 動 sit(座る)の過去, 過去分詞
- **Saturday** 名 土曜日
- **save** 動 救う
- **saw** 動 see(見る)の過去
- **say** 動 言う, 口に出す
- **scale** 名 音階
- **school** 名 学校
- **Schumann** 名 シューマン《人名。ドイツの作曲家》
- **sea** 名 海
- **second** 形 第2の, 2番目の
- **see** 動 ①見る, 見える, 見物する ②(〜と)わかる, 認識する, 経験する ③会う ④考える, 確かめる, 調べる ⑤気をつける Let me see. ええと。 See you. ではまた。 see if 〜かどうかを確かめる you see あのね, いいですか
- **seem** 動 (〜に)見える, (〜のように)思われる seem to be 〜であるように思われる
- **seen** 動 see(見る)の過去分詞
- **send** 動 送る, 手紙を出す
- **sentence** 動 判決を下す, 宣告する be sentenced to death 死刑判決を受ける
- **September** 名 9月
- **serious** 形 深刻な
- **set** 動 ①置く ②setの過去, 過去分詞 set down 〜を下に置く
- **shake** 動 揺れる, 揺さぶる, 震える
- **shall** 動 ①《Iが主語で》〜するだろう, 〜だろう ②《I以外が主語で》(…に)〜させよう, (…は)〜することになるだろう Shall we 〜? 〜しましょうか。
- **shape** 動 形づくる shaped like 〜のような形をしている
- **she** 代 彼女は[が]
- **shock** 名 衝撃, ショック 動 ショックを与える
- **shoe** 名《-s》靴
- **shook** 動 shake(振る)の過去
- **shoot** 動 (銃を)撃つ
- **should** 動 〜すべきである, 〜したほうがよい should have done 〜すべきだった(のにしなかった)《仮定法》
- **shout** 叫ぶ, 大声で言う, どなりつける
- **show** 動 ①見せる ②明らかにする
- **shut** 動 ①閉まる ②shutの過去, 過去分詞
- **sick** 形 病気の get sick 病気になる, 気分が悪くなる
- **side** 名 側, 横, そば 形 側面の, 横の from side to side 左右に
- **sign** 名 看板 動 署名する, サインする
- **simple** 形 簡単な, たんなる
- **sing** 動 (歌を)歌う, さえずる sing along 共に歌う
- **single** 形 たった1つの
- **sir** 名 あなた, 先生《目上の男性, 客などに対する呼びかけ》
- **sit** 動 ①座る, 腰掛ける ②置いてある sit still じっとしている, じっと座っている sit up straight 背筋を伸ばして座る
- **six** 名 6(の数字)
- **sixth** 形 第6番目の
- **size** 名 大きさ, サイズ
- **skin** 名 皮膚
- **sky** 名 空, 大空
- **sleep** 動 眠る, 寝る heavy with sleep (まぶたなどが)眠くて重い
- **slept** 動 sleep(眠る)の過去, 過去分詞
- **slow** 形 遅い
- **slowly** 副 ゆっくり
- **small** 形 小さい
- **small pox** 天然痘
- **smell** 動 ①(〜の)においがする

Short Stories of Kenji Miyazawa

②においをかぐ
- □ **smile** 動微笑する, にっこり笑う 名微笑, ほほえみ smile at ～に微笑みかける
- □ **smoke** 動喫煙する
- □ **snow-white** 形雪のように白い
- □ **so** 副①とても ②同様に, ～もまた ③《先行する句・節の代用》そのように, そう 接①だから, それで ②では, さて So what? それがどうした. so kind as to 親切にも～する so many 非常に多くの so that それで so ～ that 非常に～なので…
- □ **sock** 名《-s》靴下, ソックス
- □ **sol** 名ソ《音階》
- □ **soldier** 名兵士, 兵卒
- □ **some** 形①いくつかの, 多少の ②ある, 誰か, 何か 副約, いくらか いくつか ②ある人［物］たち
- □ **somebody** 代誰か, ある人
- □ **somehow** 副どことなく
- □ **someone** 代ある人, 誰か
- □ **something** 代①ある物, 何か ②いくぶん, 多少 something to do 何か～するもの
- □ **sometime** 副いつか, そのうち
- □ **sometimes** 副時々, 時たま
- □ **somewhere** 副どこかへ［に］
- □ **song** 名曲
- □ **soon** 副まもなく, すぐに, すみやかに as soon as ～するとすぐ, ～するや否や
- □ **sorry** 形気の毒に［申し訳なく］思う, 残念な feel sorry for ～をかわいそうに思う
- □ **sound** 名音, 響き 動①音がする, 鳴る ②(～のように) 思われる, (～と) 聞こえる sound like ～のように聞こえる
- □ **soup** 名汁物, スープ
- □ **south** 名南
- □ **spade** 名鋤
- □ **spark** 名火花
- □ **speak** 動話す, しゃべる speak to ～と話す
- □ **special** 形特別の, 特殊の
- □ **spent** 動 spend (～をして過ごす) の過去, 過去分詞
- □ **spoke** 動 speak (話す) の過去
- □ **spread** 動①塗る ②(うわさなどが) 広まる
- □ **spring** 名春
- □ **square** 形正方形の, 四角い
- □ **squirrel** 名リス (栗鼠)
- □ **stage** 名舞台
- □ **stamp** 動踏みつける stamp one's foot 足を踏み鳴らす
- □ **stand** 動立つ, 立っている, ある stand by そばに立つ, 待機する stand out 突き出る stand up 立ち上がる
- □ **start** 動始まる, 始める start doing ～し始める start to do ～し始める
- □ **statue** 名像
- □ **stay** 動①とどまる, 泊まる ②(～の) ままでいる stay at (場所) に泊まる stay up 起きている, 夜更かしする
- □ **steal** 動盗む
- □ **step** 名歩み, 1歩 (の距離) 動歩む, 踏む step forward 進み出る step in 介入する
- □ **stick** 名棒, スティック
- □ **still** 副①まだ, 今でも ②それでも (なお) 形静かの, 静かな keep still じっとしている sit still じっとしている, じっと座っている
- □ **stone** 名石, 小石
- □ **stood** 動 stand (立つ) の過去, 過去分詞
- □ **stop** 動①やめる, やめさせる, 止める, 止まる ②立ち止まる 名停止 stop doing ～するのをやめる
- □ **straight** 形まっすぐな, 直立［垂直］の 副一直線に, まっすぐに sit up straight 背筋を伸ばして座る

Word List

- **strange** 形 ①知らない, 見[聞き]慣れない ②奇妙な, 変わった
- **straw cape** みの《わら製のレインコート》
- **street** 名 街路, 通り
- **string** 名 弦
- **strong** 形 強い, 堅固な
- **struck** 動 strike (〜を打つ) の過去, 過去分詞
- **study** 動 学ぶ
- **stuff** 名 もの, 代物
- **stupid** 形 ばかな
- **such** 形 ①そのような, このような ②とても, 非常に **such a** そのような **such 〜 that** 非常に〜なので…
- **sudden** 形 突然の, 急な
- **suddenly** 副 突然, 急に
- **summer** 名 夏
- **sun** 名《the -》太陽, 日
- **sunny** 形 日当たりのよい, 日のさす
- **suppose** 動 ①仮定する, 推測する ②《be -d to 〜》〜することになっている, 〜するはずである
- **sure** 形 確かな, 確実な,《be - to 〜》必ず[きっと]〜する, 確信して **make sure** 確実に〜する **sure of oneself** 自信がある 副 確かに, まったく, 本当に
- **surprise** 動 驚かす 名 驚き, 不意打ち
- **surprised** 動 surprise (驚かす) の過去, 過去分詞 形 驚いた
- **sword** 名 剣, 刀
- **swum** 動 swim (泳ぐ) の過去分詞
- **symphony** 名 ①交響曲 ②交響楽団, オーケストラ

T

- **tah-tah-tee-dum** 名 タァータァーティーダン (というメロディー)
- **take** 動 ①取る, 持つ ②持って[連れて]いく, 捕らえる ③乗る ④(時間・労力を)費やす, 必要とする ⑤(ある動作を)する **It takes 〜 to** …するのに〜(時間など)がかかる **take care of** 〜の世話をする **take off** (衣服を)脱ぐ, 取り去る, 出発する **take out** 取り出す, 連れ出す **take someone home** (人)を家まで送る **take up** 取り上げる, 拾い上げる **take 〜 in** 〜を…に取り込む **take 〜 to** …するのに〜を要する, 〜を…に連れて行く
- **talk** 動 話す, 語る 名《the -》話題
- **tall** 形 背の高い
- **teach** 動 教える
- **tear** 名 涙 動 裂く, 引き離す **tear off** 引きはがす
- **tell** 動 ①話す, 言う ②教える, 知らせる **tell 〜 to** 〜に…するように言う
- **ten** 名 10(の数字)
- **terrible** 形 恐ろしい, ひどい
- **than** 接 〜よりも, 〜以上に **be no bigger than** 〜ほどの大きさだ **more than** 〜以上
- **thank** 動 感謝する, 礼を言う **thank 〜 for** 〜に対して礼を言う
- **that** 形 その, あの 代 ①それ, あれ, その[あの]人[物] ②《関係代名詞》〜である… 接 〜ということ, 〜なので, 〜だから 副 そんなに, それほど **so that** 〜するために, それで, できるように **so 〜 that** 非常に〜なので… **such 〜 that** 非常に〜なので… **That's it.** それだけのことだ。
- **the** 冠 ①その, あの ②《形容詞の前で》〜な人々 副《- + 比較級, - + 比較級》〜すればするほど…
- **theater** 名 劇場
- **their** 代 彼(女)らの, それらの
- **them** 代 彼(女)らを[に], それらを[に]
- **themselves** 代 彼(女)ら自身, それら自身

125

- **then** 副その時(に・は), それから, 次に 名その時 形その当時の **from then on** それ以来
- **there** 副①そこに[で・の], そこへ, あそこへ ②《- is [are] ~》~がある[いる] 名そこ
- **these** 代これら, これ 形これらの, この
- **they** 代①彼(女)らは[が], それらは[が] ②(一般の)人々は[が]
- **thick** 形厚い, 濃厚な
- **thin** 形薄い **disappear into thin air** 虚空に消える
- **thing** 名①物, 事 ②《-s》事情, 事柄 ③《one's -s》持ち物, 身の回り品 ④人, やつ **poor thing** 気の毒な人
- **think** 動思う, 考える **think of ~** のことを考える, ~を評価する
- **third** 形3番目の
- **thirteen** 名13(の数字)
- **this** 形①この, こちらの, これを ②今の, 現在の 代①これ, この人[物] ②今, ここ **at this** これを見て, そこで(すぐに) **this one** これ, こちら **this way** このように
- **those** 形それらの, あれらの 代それら[あれら]の人[物]
- **though** 接①~にもかかわらず, ~だが ②たとえ~でも 副しかし **as though** あたかも~のように, まるで~みたいに
- **thought** 動think(思う)の過去, 過去分詞 名考え, 意見
- **thousand** 名①1000(の数字) ②《-s》何千, 多数
- **three** 名3(の数字)
- **threw** 動throw(投げる)の過去
- **through** 前~を通して, ~中を[に], ~中 副①通して ②終わりまで, まったく, すっかり
- **throw** 動投げる, 浴びせる, ひっかける 名投げること, 投球 **throw away** ~を捨てる **throw off** (調子などを)狂わせる
- **thrown** 動throw(投げる)の過去分詞
- **ti** シ《音階》
- **tiddly-ta-ta** 名ティドゥリーターター(というメロディー)
- **tiddly-tum-tum** 名ティドリータンタン(というメロディー)
- **tie** 動結ぶ, 束縛する 名ネクタイ **tie up** 拘束する
- **tiger** 名トラ(虎)
- **tight** 副堅く, しっかりと
- **time** 名①時, 時間, 歳月 ②時期 ③期間 ④時代 ⑤回, 倍 **all the time** ずっと, いつも **by the time ~する**時までに **by this time** もうすでに **every time** ~するときはいつも **from time to time** ときどき **in time** 正しいテンポで **in time with** ~に合わせて **next time** 次回に
- **tired** 動tire(疲れる)の過去, 過去分詞 形①疲れた, くたびれた ②あきた, うんざりした **be tired of** ~に飽きて[うんざりして]いる
- **tiring** 形疲れる, 骨の折れる
- **to** 前①《方向・変化》~へ, ~に, ~の方へ ②《程度・時間》~まで ③《適合・付加・所属》~に ④《- + 動詞の原形》~するために[の], ~する, ~すること
- **today** 名今日
- **together** 副①一緒に, ともに ②同時に
- **told** 動tell(話す)の過去, 過去分詞
- **tomato** 名トマト
- **tomorrow** 副明日は
- **tongue** 名舌
- **tonight** 副今夜は
- **too** 副①~も(また) ②あまりに~すぎる, とても~ **too much** 過度の, やりすぎの
- **took** 動take(取る)の過去
- **top** 名最上部, 上端
- **tore** 動tear(裂く)の過去

Word List

- **total** 名全体, 合計
- **toward** 前《運動の方向・位置》～の方へ, ～に向かって
- **town** 名町, 都市
- **train** 動訓練する
- **Träumerei** 名トロイメライ《楽曲》
- **travel** 動旅行する
- **tree** 名木, 樹木
- **trial** 名裁判　**put on trial** 裁判にかける
- **tried** 動try（試みる）の過去, 過去分詞
- **trouble** 名①困難, 迷惑, もめごと ②心配, 苦労　動①悩ます, 心配させる ②迷惑をかける
- **true** 形本当の, 真の, 確かな
- **truly** 副心から, 誠実に　**Yours truly** 敬具《堅い手紙の結び文句》
- **trumpet** 名ラッパ, トランペット
- **truth** 名真理, 事実
- **try** 動①やってみる, 試みる ②努力する, 努める　名試み, 試し　**give it a try** 試しにやってみる
- **turn** 動①ひっくり返す, 向かう, 向ける ②（～に）なる,（～に）変える　**turn around** 振り向く　**turn off**（照明などを）消す　**turn red** 赤くなる　**turn to** ～の方を向く　**turn up** 上向きに曲げる
- **twice** 副2度, 2回
- **two** 名2（の数字）

U

- **under** 前～の下[に]
- **understand** 動理解する, わかる
- **uneasy** 形不安な
- **university** 名（総合）大学
- **unless** 接～しなければ
- **until** 前～まで（ずっと）　接～の時まで, ～するまで
- **up** 副①上へ, 上がって, 北へ ②立って, 近づいて ③向上して, 増して　前①～の上（の方）へ, 高い方へ ②（道）に沿って　形上向きの, 上りの　**be up to** ～次第である　**up to** ①～まで ②～次第である
- **upset** 形動揺して, 取り乱して
- **us** 代私たちを[に]
- **use** 動使う, 用いる
- **used** 動use（使う）の過去　**used to**《be-》～に慣れる
- **usual** 形通常の, いつもの　**as usual** いつものように

V

- **vegetable** 名野菜
- **Venus Orchestra** 金星音楽団
- **very** 副とても, 非常に, まったく　形本当の, きわめて, まさしくその
- **vinegar** 名酢, ビネガー
- **violin** 名バイオリン
- **visit** 動訪問する
- **visitor** 名訪問客
- **voice** 名声

W

- **wagon** 名荷馬車
- **wait** 動待つ,《-for ～》～を待つ　**Wait a minute.** ちょっと待って。
- **wake up** 起きる, 目を覚ます
- **walk** 動歩く　**walk away** 立ち去る, 遠ざかる　**walk off** 立ち去る　**walk to** ～まで歩いて行く
- **wall** 名壁
- **want** 動ほしい, 望む, ～したい, ～してほしい
- **warm** 形暖かい
- **was** 動《beの第1・第3人称単数現在am, isの過去》～であった,（～に）

Short Stories of Kenji Miyazawa

いた[あった]
- **wash** 動洗う **wash off** 洗い落とす
- **waste** 動浪費する 形廃棄された **waste paper** 古紙
- **watch** 動①じっと見る, 見物する ②注意[用心]する, 監視する **watch over** 見守る, 見張る
- **water** 名①水 ②(川・湖・海などの)多量の水
- **way** 名①道, 通り道 ②方向, 距離 ③方法, 手段 ④習慣 **all the way** はるばる, わざわざ **lead the way** 先に立って導く **on the way** 途中で **this way** このように, こっちに, こちらの方へ
- **we** 代私たちは[が]
- **week** 名週, 1週間
- **welcome** 形歓迎される
- **well** 副①うまく, 上手に ②十分に, よく, かなり 間へえ, まあ, ええと 形健康な **as well** なお, 同様に **well done** よくやった **well enough** かなり上手に
- **went** 動 go (行く)の過去
- **were** 動《be の2人称単数・複数の過去》~であった, (~に)いた[あった]
- **west** 名西 副西へ
- **wet** 形湿った
- **what** 代①何が[を・に] ②《関係代名詞》~するところのもの[こと] 形①何の, どんな ②なんと ③~するだけの 副いかに, どれほど **So what?** それがどうした。 **what on earth** 一体全体
- **whatever** 代《関係代名詞》どんなこと[もの]が~とも
- **when** 副①いつ ②《関係副詞》~するところの, ~するとその時, ~するとき 接~の時, ~するとき 代いつ
- **where** 副①どこに[で] ②《関係副詞》~するところの, そしてそこで, ~するところ 接~なところに[へ], ~するところに[へ] 代①どこ, どの点 ②~するところの

- **while** 接①~の間(に), ~する間(に) ②一方, ~なのに 名しばらくの間, 一定の時 **all the while** その間ずっと **for a while** しばらくの間, 少しの間
- **whisker** 名《-s》ほおひげ
- **whistle** 動(口)笛を吹く
- **whistle-like** 形口笛のような
- **white** 形①白い, (顔色などが)青ざめた
- **who** 代①誰が[は], どの人 ②《関係代名詞》~するところの(人)
- **whole** 形全体の, すべての
- **why** 副①なぜ, どうして ②《関係副詞》~するところの(理由) **Why don't you ~?** ~したらどうだい, ~しませんか
- **wide** 形幅の広い 副広く, 大きく開いて
- **wild** 形①野生の ②荒れ果てた
- **wild cat** ヤマネコ
- **will** 助~だろう, ~しよう, する(つもりだ)
- **wind** 名風
- **window** 名窓, 窓ガラス
- **windy** 形風の吹く, 風の強い
- **wipe** 動~をふく, ぬぐう
- **wise** 形賢そうな
- **wish** 動望む, 願う, (~であればよいと)思う
- **with** 前①《同伴・付随・所属》~と一緒に, ~を身につけて, ~とともに ②《様態》~(の状態)で, ~して ③《手段・道具》~で, ~を使って
- **without** 前~なしで, ~しないで
- **woke** 動 wake (目が覚める)の過去
- **wonder** 動不思議に思う, (~かしらと)思う **wonder if** ~ではないかと思う
- **wonderful** 形すばらしい, すてきな

Word List

- □ **won't** will notの短縮形
- □ **wood** 名 ①《しばしば-s》森, 林 ② 木材, まき
- □ **word** 名 ①語, 単語 ②ひと言
- □ **wording** 名 言い回し, 表現
- □ **wore** 動 wear (着ている)の過去
- □ **work** 動 作用する, うまくいく 名 仕事, 職 **work out** うまくいく, 何とかなる
- □ **worker** 名 労働者
- □ **worried** 動 worry (心配する)の過去, 過去分詞 形 心配そうな, 不安げな
- □ **worry** 動 心配する[させる]
- □ **worst** 形《the –》最も悪い, いちばんひどい
- □ **would** 動《willの過去》①~するだろう, ~するつもりだ ②~したものだ **Would you like ~?** ~はいかがですか。 **would like to** ~したいと思う **would love to do** ~したい
- □ **wow** 間《驚きなどを表して》わあ!, へえ!
- □ **write** 動 書く, 手紙を書く **write down** 書き留める
- □ **writing** 動 write (書く)の現在分詞 名 著述, 筆跡
- □ **written** 動 write (書く)の過去分詞
- □ **wrong** 形 間違った, 調子が悪い 副 間違って **be wrong with** (~にとって)よくない
- □ **wrote** 動 write (書く)の過去

Y

- □ **yard** 名 庭
- □ **year** 名 年, 1年 **all year** 一年中, 一年を通して
- □ **yell** 動 大声をあげる, わめく
- □ **yellow** 形 黄色の
- □ **yes** 副 はい, そうです
- □ **yesterday** 名 昨日 **day before yesterday**《おとといに》
- □ **yet** 副 ①《否定文で》まだ~(ない[しない]) ②《肯定文で》まだ, 今もなお **yet another** さらにもう一つの
- □ **you** 代 ①あなた(方)は[が], あなた(方)を[に] ②(一般に)人は **you know** ご存知のとおり, あのね, ほら **you see** ほら, あのね, いいですか
- □ **young** 形 若い, 幼い, 青年の
- □ **your** 代 あなた(方)の
- □ **yours** 代 あなた(方)のもの **Yours truly** 敬具《堅い手紙の結び文句》
- □ **yourself** 代 あなた自身

English Conversational Ability Test
国際英語会話能力検定

● E-CATとは…
英語が話せるようになるためのテストです。インターネットベースで、30分であなたの発話力をチェックします。

www.ecatexam.com

● iTEP®とは…
世界各国の企業、政府機関、アメリカの大学300校以上が、英語能力判定テストとして採用。オンラインによる90分のテストで文法、リーディング、リスニング、ライティング、スピーキングの5技能をスコア化。iTEP®は、留学、就職、海外赴任などに必要な、世界に通用する英語力を総合的に評価する画期的なテストです。

www.itepexamjapan.com

ラダーシリーズ
Short Stories of Kenji Miyazawa
宮沢賢治短編集

2016年12月23日　第1刷発行
2021年 9月10日　第2刷発行

原著者　宮沢 賢治

発行者　浦　晋亮

発行所　IBCパブリッシング株式会社
　　　　〒162-0804 東京都新宿区中里町29番3号
　　　　菱秀神楽坂ビル9F
　　　　Tel. 03-3513-4511　Fax. 03-3513-4512
　　　　www.ibcpub.co.jp

© IBC Publishing, Inc. 2016

印刷　株式会社シナノパブリッシングプレス
装丁　伊藤 理恵
カバーイラスト　topilipa/Shutterstock.com　本文イラスト　山田 勇男
組版データ　Sabon Roman + Georgia Bold

落丁本・乱丁本は、小社宛にお送りください。送料小社負担にてお取り替えいたします。
本書の無断複写（コピー）は著作権法上での例外を除き禁じられています。

Printed in Japan
ISBN 978-4-7946-0453-8